Dr. Michael J. Holosko
BRENDA SCHREIBER

On
COMMUNICATION

195

195

On
COMMUNICATION

Listening, Reading, Speaking, and Writing

Richard Swanson • Charles Marquardt
Madison Area Technical College

GLENCOE PRESS
A division of Benziger Bruce & Glencoe, Inc.
Beverly Hills

Collier Macmillan Publishers
London

Glencoe Press
A division of Benziger Bruce & Glencoe, Inc.
8701 Wilshire Boulevard
Beverly Hills, California 90211

Collier-Macmillan Canada, Ltd.

Library of Congress catalog card number: 73-7370

2 3 4 5 6 7 8 9 PPr 80 79 78 77

Contents

Preface

WE ARE LIVING in a time of change—social, political, and economic. One factor that will play a critical role in our ability to adjust to a changing world is our ability to communicate—a process that involves not only writing and speaking, but the companion acts of reading and listening as well.

This book is not about grammar, punctuation, the after-dinner speech, or parliamentary procedure. It focuses on the day-by-day situations in which people must understand one another. Not that grammar, punctuation, and the rest have no place, but too often, they are studied as though they had no connection with the give-and-take of people in everyday life. We put this everyday exchange of ideas at the forefront, incorporating insights from psychology, the mass media, marketing, and semantics.

Most importantly, this book provides not only a new but also a *unifying* focus. For too long, English and speech have been taught as separate skills, in different departments by different instructors using different books. This insulation strengthened the notion that the skills were unrelated, a notion we try to combat here. With a basic communication model serving as a key to the communication process, we trace the relationships between writer, speaker, listener, and reader. Once the student understands the process and the relationships, he can go on to more highly structured and complex communication exercises, and increase his effectiveness as a communicator.

This book might be used in either single-semester or full-year courses, but it is not intended to be an all-purpose text. Most teachers will want to complement it with additional readings. It is designed to be a core text, around which supplementary material can be arranged.

The amount and use of time spent with the book depends largely on the teacher's approach and the needs of the class. *On Communication* provides enough exercises to last a year, a semester, or a part of a semester. These exercises, we have found, are flexible and wide-ranging enough so they can be used by students at different levels of achievement. A teacher's manual is available, containing review tests, additional background information on communication theory, suggested course approaches, and a bibliography of the materials that went into the making of the text.

Finally, we must acknowledge the encouragement and help offered by friends, colleagues, students, and our publisher. Their assistance has been invaluable. We owe a special debt to Mike Irwin, who provided unflagging support and perceptive suggestions in the early stage of the book, and to Jenny Alkire at Glencoe Press, who did likewise in the final stages.

1

The Value of Good Communication

- VALUE TO YOU AS A WORKER

- VALUE TO YOU AS A SOCIAL INDIVIDUAL

- VALUE TO YOU AS A CITIZEN

ALMOST EVERYONE at one time or another has been told that good communication is valuable. Perhaps it was a teacher, or one of your parents, who first tried to explain that it was essential for you to communicate your thoughts as clearly as possible. At the time, you probably accepted the idea without really understanding what good communication meant, much less why it should be an important skill for you to cultivate. Yet today you find yourself taking a course dealing with that very subject; you are surrounded by messages about "credibility gaps" in newspapers and on TV; you see movies and plays that focus on the human crises that often result from a failure to communicate. Is all this concern with communication a short-lived phenomenon, of passing interest only? Or is there something more involved, something worth an entire book on our part and a lot of thought on yours?

Value to You as a Worker

Suppose we take a closer look at these questions, using typical situations as our examples. First, a practical one, in the business world you might be entering shortly. The scene is a custom furniture manufacturing company. It is midmorning and work is proceeding as usual. Mr. Wyngard, the company billing clerk, is sending out the customers' bills. A good deal of his work has already been done for him by computer. Machines have printed the amounts and typed in the addresses. Some of the accounts are overdue. To these Mr. Wyngard attaches a form letter notifying the customer of this fact.

In another part of the office Miss Ayres is writing a technical report on several materials the company is considering for the upholstery of a new line of chairs. In contrast to Mr. Wyngard's task, hers takes a lot of thought. The textile consultants in the company have given her the alternatives, and now she must interpret them for Mr. Dickinson, the president of the company. Mr. Dickinson was in on the preliminary planning but has been too busy recently to be directly involved with this project. Miss Ayres' task, therefore, is to describe the advantages and disadvantages of the various materials to Mr. Dickinson as briefly as possible. He needs an accurate summary of the essentials, nothing more and nothing less. Miss Ayres must serve as a liaison between the consultants and the president.

In a private office in the building Mr. Dickinson is having a conference with one of the company's best salesmen, who is going out this morning to talk with a group of executives about a new line of office furniture the company designed and built some months ago. Mr. Dickinson has chosen this salesman because the man relates very well to a variety of people. Between them they are deciding on the best approach in presenting the new line. Each of them discusses various methods. Ideas are accepted and discarded on both sides. As soon as the salesman leaves, Mr. Dickinson relaxes a moment. "We lost a week on this project," he thinks, "because I didn't stress the cost factor enough to our designers. I was thinking of a full suite of furniture for under $10,000. They were thinking of $8000 until we finally sat down and discussed the whole matter over coffee."

So goes a typical morning in a typical business. What can we conclude about the value of good communication from this example?

The duties of Mr. Wyngard reflect the current widespread practice of handling many written communications by machine and by standardized, printed forms. His predecessor might have written out the bills and follow-up letters for overdue accounts, but his role is that of a sorter or checker.

Miss Ayres and Mr. Dickinson give us a different view of communication. From them we see that as a person moves up the ladder of job success the need for communication proficiency, spoken and written, increases. Time is a factor in these jobs so that communication has to be to the point. Communication must be accurate also because money is involved. At the top level of the company, Mr. Dickinson's task of communicating is very complex, because he must deal with many people, his designers, the technical writer Miss Ayres, his salesmen, and indirectly his customers.

One conclusion to be drawn from this business situation is that communication at the unskilled level has been somewhat simplified with the introduction of computers. However, at the technical and management levels the individual's skill as a communicator is still as important as ever, if not more so. From your own point of view, then, the ability to communicate well represents a valuable asset in the job market.

Value to You as a Social Individual

But suppose we look at an entirely different situation: three students sitting in a drugstore booth talking about a movie they have seen the previous night. The movie apparently caused mixed reactions, for a real debate is going on. Tom, on the one side, is arguing that the movie doesn't have a good plot. Norman disagrees, saying that the unstructured plot helps convey the point of the film. The conversation goes as follows.

TOM: But a film ought to have something happen in it, and this one doesn't. The people get up in the morning. Then there's more footage on what they do during the day. Then they come home at night. I mean nothing happens.

NORMAN: Right. Which is why it's good. They're people without promise. They do little, think less, and just exist. That's the idea behind the film.

Looking on and listening to this conversation is Lois, a third student, who has not yet made up her mind about the film but finds herself tending to agree with Norman. "He gets his ideas across so well," she thinks to herself. "I wonder if I'm not more convinced by the way he says things than by what he says."

Her observation is a perceptive one. Norman does express himself well, and his argument is certainly strengthened by his choice of words and manner of speaking. In any case, his listener has been impressed, illustrating another result of skillful communication: increased personal prestige.

Value to You as a Citizen

A third situation illustrates still another aspect of communication. On a street corner in an American city two people are talking about an upcoming election. One of them remarks that he supports the candidate running for reelection, who stands for law and order. He had once written him a letter asking for streetlights in his neighborhood because the dark streets were dangerous at night, and the lights had been installed. When the other man says that he too considers law and order the major issue, both men automatically conclude they are voting for the same candidate. They are greatly surprised to learn, then, that they are voting for two different people. A discussion follows centered around each candidate's interpretation of law and order. As a result of this discussion each man becomes better informed about the other's views. They may not agree any more than they did before, but at least they have enlarged their perspective.

This particular example is far from insignificant. The open discussion of political issues is vital to a democratic form of government. Had the two men in the foregoing situation not bothered to exchange views, each would have been voting blindly, in a sense, convinced that his candidate was the best choice, without hearing either positive opinions on the opposition or negative opinions on his candidate.

This example also illustrates another factor, just as important as open discussion to the successful operation of a democracy. That factor is the ability of the people to express their wishes to elected officials, who must pass legislation reflecting both majority and minority views. Only by having good communication with the people as a whole, and with fellow lawmakers, can our representatives carry out their task successfully.

Summary

Effective communication yields both economic returns and personal prestige for the individual who practices it. Equally important, good communication is vital to a democratic society.

Assignments

1. Interview three people in business or industry. Find out from them the specific communication skills required in a particular job that interests you. Find out also the time spent in communicating and how this time can be broken down into speaking, writing, listening, and reading.

2. Take a survey of five or six friends and five or six older adult acquaintances. Answer the following questions:

a. Which of these factors has most influenced your opinions on public issues—your friends, leaders in your peer group, your parents, the mass media, national leaders, or leaders of organizations to which you belong? Rank these in order of importance.

b. Are there differences in the group responses between your age group and the older adults? Report your findings in a short oral or written report.

2

What Is Good Communication?

I F YOU'RE AT ALL familiar with classical music, you may have heard of a work by Charles Ives entitled "The Unanswered Question." That title could very well serve as a subtitle for this chapter, for it attempts to answer the question "What is good communication?" and that answer is not easy to determine.

It would be nice to dash to the dictionary at this point, thumb through it to find the term we're looking for, and settle back in the confidence that we had fifteen words which summed up good communication. But somehow the definition of "communication" supplied by Webster's—"a process by which meanings are exchanged by individuals"—just doesn't fill the bill. Good communication is one of those concepts that requires some analysis and does not fit neatly into anyone's mental computer for quick future use. Unlike math, where two and two equals four, in communication two and two might equal three, four and a half, or none of these.

Some General Principles

Rather than admit defeat before we start, let us take a common-sense approach to the problem. No one needs to do any research to recognize a few basic elements of good communication. We need only consider the characteristics that different communication situations have in common to discover these principles.

Good communication is directed toward a specific purpose. This is number one on the list, and it seems obvious. Everyone who communicates, in written or spoken form, has some specific purpose in mind: to invite a friend to a wedding, to persuade someone to buy life insurance, to inform a company about how poorly a new lawn mower works, to request a deferment from the armed services—the list is endless. Every situation in which communication is involved should lead to a specific goal.

Good communication is directed toward a specific audience. Everyone who has something to communicate must have someone to communicate with. It may be one person or many, but regardless of numbers the audience can be described in specific terms. Is the audience friendly, indifferent, or hostile? Is it young, middle-aged, or older? Perhaps it is an acquaintance who owns a car like yours. It might be a teacher who cringes over split infinitives in themes.

All of these people have assorted traits and beliefs of which you should be aware. Suppose for example that you are a ticket chairman of a theater organization. If you expect to sell tickets to the three groups just mentioned—the young, middle-aged, and older—your letter of appeal will have to be different for each age bracket. The younger group may like the experimental staging of the plays, the middle-aged group may be more interested in the subtle development of the plot, the older people may be more interested in some of the older characters. The essential point is that each group has to be approached in a different way.

Good communication anticipates difficulty. Once you have accepted the principle of a specific audience, it might be tempting to conclude that there will be no difficulty in communicating. In other words, if you plan your communication to appeal to that audience, then why should there be any confusion? But it's not quite that simple. Take this chapter for an illustration. It is directed toward a specific audience, a group of students—and you in particular—all having some need for better communication skills. It would seem, then, that we should have no problem in explaining the material. But of course there are many kinds of students, and we've tried to keep this in mind throughout: for example, the person who likes neat definitions. We have tried to anticipate his natural wish to formulate a simple definition for good communication by warning him in advance that we plan to approach the subject differently.

Another illustration of this principle, one familiar to all of us, is asking someone for directions in an unfamiliar neighborhood. "Go about a mile north out of town," the person might have said, "and when you get to the third crossroad, turn left." But the person failed to anticipate our uncertainty when the road suddenly veered northeast. And the person forgot all about those two *gravel* crossroads that appeared before the first *hard* crossroad. At a time like this, the phrase "You can't miss it!" sounds ludicrous.

Good communication is complete and to the point. If you are going to communicate well, it is not enough to cover most of the subject. Rather, you must be sure that you have left no room for misunderstanding. If you do not tell the whole story, your listener or reader will be left with an opinion based on insufficient information. At the same time, you must keep to the point, and avoid cluttering up your message with irrelevant details. You've probably heard speakers who got sidetracked talking about subordinate points, and never seemed to get to the main idea. After a few minutes of listening you lost interest entirely, and your mind just tuned out. By contrast, what a pleasure it is to watch a top comedian telling a joke. Every word contributes to the total effect. The diversions are carefully planned for meaning and suspense. He gets into the punch line easily. And we all laugh—in appreciation of his skill at manipulating words, as well as at the joke itself.

Good communication is clear and precise. This principle is related to the previous four. If your communication is aimed at a specific purpose and a specific audience, if it includes all essential information without unnecessary embroidery, then it should be clear and precise. The ideal is not a minimum or maximum number of words, but an optimum: all the words needed to give an accurate picture of a given situation, and no more. In addition, especially in formal written or spoken communications, it's important to find the *right* word to convey a particular idea. Try to avoid being the kind of communicator whose message is punctuated by the phrase "Or-Something-Like-That." He's always on the verge of the right word or concept but never finds it, with the result that the other person has to fill in the gaps and make the connections, an exasperating experience.

Good communication is personal. Anyone who thinks he is successful in communicating just because he has adhered to all the previous principles is in for a surprise. He's neglecting a very important dimension of the communication process—the human one. The excellent salesman does not ignore this. He is aware that it is not enough to be purposeful, specific, clear, and precise. He knows that people want to be treated as individuals with personalities. They want others to notice their new spring clothes, their particular slant on life, their favorite pastimes. Anyone who is oblivious to these matters runs the risk of being a cold-fish communicator, hence a less-than-successful one.

Good communication is tactful. Just being personable is not the whole story either, for there may be times when you want to *persuade* someone to do something he perhaps is not eager to do. You may need his vote. You may want him to keep his kids quiet. The best way to get him to consider your viewpoint in such cases is to communicate tactfully. Such phrases as "I don't have all the answers to this question, but," and "I like to think everyone is open-minded enough to consider this proposal fairly" help create the right psychological climate for free exchange of opinion. And this is essential, for most research on persuasion shows that people cannot be influenced unless they feel comfortable with the persuader. In other words, it won't help you any to come on like a pro football linebacker.

A key word to remember in regard to this principle is *sincerity.* If the speaker or writer genuinely attempts to see things as his audience does, then his chances of getting through to them are good. If on the other hand he is merely paying lip service to the idea of tact, saying the "right" things without first acquiring some kind of rapport with his audience, his chances are not much better than if he were blatantly hostile. Tact, then, as we are using the word, has two meanings: the keen awareness of audience beliefs, and the sincere attempt to create a good climate for persuasion.

Good communication is appropriate. Implicit in all the principles mentioned so far is another: your message must be worded so it is appropriate for the situation and people involved. For example, suppose your friend Charlie has been stopped by a policeman, who now approaches Charlie's car. Charlie has a choice of two initial statements. He can say, "What's the trouble, officer?" or he can say, "What's up, pig?" In either case he is to the point, clear, specific, and personal. In the second case, however, his choice of words is far from appropriate. He has been much too informal for what turns out to be a very formal occasion. As a result he may have to be present on another very formal occasion, his courtroom trial.

It is possible, of course, to go to the other extreme. If Tom is discussing a book with his friend Gwen, and he remarks "It seemed to me that the protagonist displayed an excessively neurotic preoccupation with horticulture," the conversation is likely to stop right there. Tom's approach would be fine in a term paper, but it's much too formal for casual conversation. Gwen would be a lot more interested if he said simply, "It's the story of a man who cares more about flowers than he does about people."

Now that we've presented some basic principles, it might seem logical to formulate a definition of good communication. But in order to clarify these principles further, we're going to look at the communication process from a different angle first; then a definition will be forthcoming. This next section, in which we describe what is known as a communication model,[1] will provide the framework for the remaining chapters in your text.

A Model of the Process

We begin, then, a second time, with you. In any act of communication you are either a sender or receiver. You are part of the communicative process, an exchange between at least two people. You react to something and attempt to share it; or someone else reacts to a situation, passes his impression on, and asks you to respond.

For now, let us assume it is you who acts as a sender. You are in the library of your school and notice a girl come in and sit at another table. You are immediately attracted to her; she wears bright-colored clothing and walks in such a way that she stands out from everyone else around her. Not only that, she's carrying a science-fiction novel by Isaac Asimov, an author you read regularly.

1. In arriving at our communication model we have borrowed from A. T. Weaver and O. G. Ness's *The Fundamentals and Forms of Speech* (New York, 1963).

As a result of these favorable impressions you decide to scribble a note to your best friend, studying next to you. You want to share your excitement with him, to tell him about the girl as best as you can. You become a sender, and he will be your receiver. We can diagram this idea in the following way.

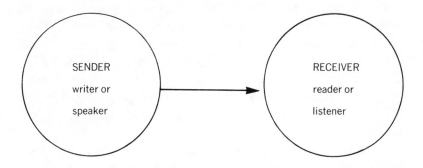

This looks relatively uncomplicated. However, it is oversimplified, for we can identify another step in the process which the diagram does not allow for. This is the formulation of the precise idea, bit of information, or picture of the girl you will try to convey to your friend. "Hm," you think, "she's attractive and is a science-fiction fan too. How do I get this across?"

We identify this idea, information, or picture as the *message*, that which you want to transmit to someone. Ideally it is the sum total, or a good summary, of all the impressions you had. Our diagram of the communication process now looks like this.

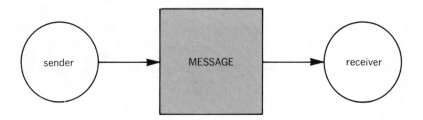

This looks relatively simple also, but it is still incomplete. For before your friend can begin to grasp the message, another step must take place. You have to "code" that idea, bit of information, or picture. Roughly translated "code" means "language," that is, a system of spoken or written symbols called *words*; or "para-language," which refers to tone of voice, posture, diagrams, and so on. In this case you put down on paper: "Third table over—burgundy/yellow shirt and thin gold bracelets. A sci-fi fan too. Wow!" In sending your message, you use various words to represent places, objects, characteristics, and value judgments. *Third table over* are words that indicate the place where your attention is focused. *Burgundy/yellow shirt and thin gold bracelets* is your coded phrase for attractive dress colors and items. *A sci-fi fan* indicates the girl's interest in the science-fiction book. *Wow* stands for your positive, excited attitude.

It is easy to pass lightly over this code factor because we are familiar with the words in the statement. But suppose your friend is an Oriental student who is not yet fluent in English. The importance of code now becomes obvious. You may have to offer alternate symbols, synonyms that he could recognize. You may have to spell out *science fiction* in order for him to understand. Even if he is not a foreigner, though, your code may still cause difficulty. For instance, *third table over* isn't very clear, so you may want to resort to another kind of code—drawing a quick sketch of the section of the library you're sitting in, marking an X on it where the girl is located.

It is evident that the code factor deserves a place in our diagram of the communication process:

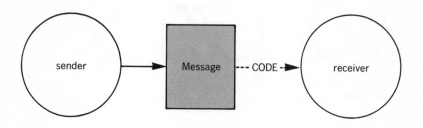

WHAT IS GOOD COMMUNICATION?

Our model is beginning to look more complete. But to be accurate we must include still another item with a name borrowed from the language of science: the channel. For your purposes this means either the air waves that carry your voice, or the piece of paper with words or drawings that convey the coded message. Once you have coded the message, the next step is to send it over a channel to your friend.

You may be asking yourself now, "Why bring this in, since it's so obvious?" This is a logical question. Channel is emphasized here because it is the *only* part of the process that is substantially different for writing than it is for speaking. Yet many people seem to think that communicating in speech and writing are separate procedures, requiring separate sets of skills. How often, for example, have you heard someone say, "I can't make myself understood in writing as I can when I speak." Yet common sense tells us that this logic won't hold up. There *is* a difference in writing and speaking. That difference is the channel; and you may have to adjust the coding of your message to conform to the channel you use (as you did in writing the note to your friend in the library). But whether you use air waves or paper and ink, all the other basic communication elements will remain the same. You still try to get across your reaction by identifying an impression, putting it into a message, and then coding it. Thus, if you have trouble communicating in a written message, chances are your spoken messages are not coming across as well as you might think.

The diagram now looks like this:

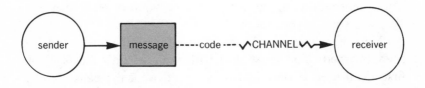

Thus far, the diagram illustrates the first half of the communication process: transmittal and reception of the message. The second half of the process is called *feedback*: the receiver's instant or delayed reaction to that message. Figure 1 shows the diagram with feedback added.

As the diagram illustrates, it is feedback that makes the communication process an exchange rather than simply a one-way street. Feedback tells the sender if he has succeeded in getting his message across. The receiver's response, negative or positive, supplies the sharing element we mentioned earlier. This feedback may be no more than your friend's smile as he sees the girl you have described. It may be a statement answering yours: "Wow to you maybe, not me." Whatever his response, however, it helps you to appraise the effectiveness of your communication.

Two other points about feedback are worth making. One is that, while the diagram indicates that it occurs as a specific step in the process, it actually flows continuously from the start of the communicative act—especially in speaking. The sender gets clues as to how well he is succeeding; the receiver feeds back reactions or tries to anticipate whatever point the sender is trying to make. (More about this in the next chapter.)

Second, as the diagram indicates, feedback reflects a process of revision that takes place in the receiver's mind. You sent your friend a message describing a girl and giving your reaction: "Wow!" As your friend read the message, he interpreted it and responded to it, all in the space of a few seconds. First he *decoded* the message—translated it to get to the meaning underlying your words ("He'd like to get to know the girl reading the Asimov book"). Then he *reacted* to it—decided whether or not he agreed with you ("She's OK, I guess, but she's not my type"). Last, he *encoded* his feedback message—put his reaction into words, corresponding to the words of your original message: "Wow to you, maybe, not me."

Now the whole process repeats itself, with the sender-receiver roles reversed. You must deal with your friend's message, but first you'll need to decode it—figure out what it means, exactly. Does he mean that the girl doesn't dress conservatively enough for him? Or does he mean that he doesn't like science fiction, and therefore he could care less that she happens to be reading

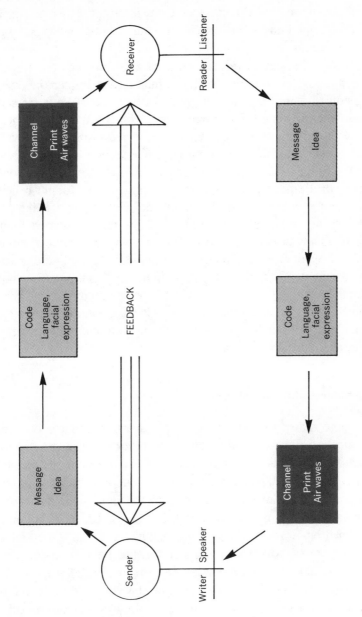

Figure 1. The Function of Feedback

Asimov? Perhaps his reaction is based on other characteristics you haven't noticed. Until you have interpreted his feedback, you will not know how accurately your original message came across to him.

This brings us to the last element affecting the communicative process: interference, or those factors that hinder the transmission of a message at any point. In the case of your message about the girl, interference may result from your friend's lack of sleep the night before; he's tired, he's in a bad mood, and your enthusiasm rubs him the wrong way. It may be your badly scribbled writing, which prevents him from making out the words *sci-fi fan*. Perhaps you forgot that, unlike you, he doesn't believe that people who wear bright colors and wild outfits are likely to be exciting and creative. The kinds of interference involved here are relatively easy to deal with. Others, sometimes almost impossible to overcome, may relate to an individual's background and environment. Certain ingrown prejudices, or simply his whole way of looking at life, could lead to major communication breakdowns in his relations with others. All these interferences affect our ability to function at each stage of the communicative process, as Figure 2 indicates.

The Answerable Question

We now return to that unanswerable question about good communication. There is, after all, a definition we can give. Good communication is the exchange of ideas, information, and experiences which takes into account the general principles we outlined plus the elements and steps in the diagrams. It is not a simple definition by any standard, but that is because communication itself is never simple. If one could restrict all the variables in the process—the sender and receiver, the message, code, channel, feedback, and interference—then a concise definition would be possible. But that is just wishful thinking; people can't be reduced to a formula, so it's not surprising that communication can't either.

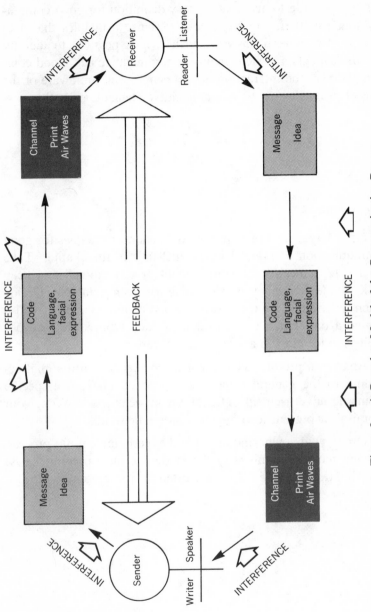

Figure 2.   A Complete Model of the Communication Process,
Including Interference

Summary

It is not possible to arrive at an easy definition for good communication. But there are some commonsense principles that help us toward a general answer. Further, it is possible to identify certain elements and steps in any communicative act. Good communication is the interaction of two people who are aware of the general principles or the communicative elements or both.

Assignments

1. On a large sheet of paper list the general principles for good communication mentioned in the first half of the chapter. Take this list to a meeting of your student or city council and keep track of the frequency of violations for each principle. Decide which individuals are the best and worst communicators; try also to give a one-sentence description of each failure. Report your findings to the class in a written or oral report.

2. Analyze a product advertisement you receive in the mail according to the general principles mentioned above. Be specific about the advertisement's strengths and weaknesses. Write your appraisal or present it to the class in a concise talk.

3. Draw your own diagram of the communication process, showing the shortcomings of the model we have presented. Use your diagram as the basis for a written or oral presentation.

3
Sender–Receiver

Now let's explore the relationship between sender and receiver and examine the roles of feedback, image, and empathy in making communication successful.

Feedback: How Am I Doing?

Remember the communication model? Feedback, the receiver's reaction to the sender's message, made the process a circular one. It's this reciprocity, this two-way network, that makes communication effective. Remember the last time someone yawned while you were telling a joke? Recall when your term paper came back with criticisms scribbled in the margin? Only when you got this feedback did you begin to understand how your message got through.

You should keep in mind, however, that there are several different kinds of feedback: a response may be immediate or delayed, thoughtful or impulsive. Does the receiver answer you on the spot, or is there a time lapse between your sending and his replying? Immediate feedback implies that your audience is *with you* when you are sending the message. Does the receiver make hasty assumptions about your message, and pass them on to you right away? Or does he pause to consider what he has heard or read before replying?

We need to be aware of these kinds of feedback if we are to move easily from the role of speaking sender to the role of writing sender (and vice versa). For example, the speaker's message is fed back to him immediately, in the form of audience cues such as drumming fingers, hostile looks, expressions of surprise, laughter, incessant coughing, or spontaneous applause. In response to these cues, the speaker can correct or deviate occasionally from his planned message, adding explanatory details if his receiver seems confused and stressing a point if the receiver shows unusual interest.

For the writer feedback is usually more delayed, with a good possibility of the receiver being some distance from the sender (you write a letter to someone and get an answer two weeks later). But chances are this feedback has been more carefully considered than an immediate, live response. Why? Because the reader can sometimes be more honest if you're not there, because he is under little obligation to respond momentarily, and because he has a permanent copy of your message (the letter) to go back to. In these circumstances he can weigh and consider your thoughts (and his reactions) longer; and he can check his reply against your prose as many times as he wants, something the listener can't do because he could refer to your spoken words only as long as his memory retained them.

As a sender, then, neither speaker nor writer is in a particularly ideal position. The speaker has a time advantage and a live audience, but the feedback may not be as reliable because it's spur of the moment. The impact of feedback received by the writer is lessened through the passage of time, but that feedback may be more carefully considered than the instant response of the speaker's audience. In either case, however, the kind of feedback is not so important as the fact that it exists in the first place. As we have pointed out, feedback completes the exchange of thought between two individuals. With feedback they become communicators.

Image: Who Am I? Who Are You?
What Do We Think of Each Other?

How successfully we communicate is often determined by the images, or mental pictures, we have of ourselves and one another in certain situations. These images are a vital factor in the way the sender and receiver interact.

Let's probe this concept of image more deeply. The image you have of your school while you are describing it in a letter to a friend is far different from the one you might have the same evening as you cheer your school team at a basketball or football game. The image you had of your parents when they imposed a strict curfew upon you in high school gave way to quite a different one when they promised you a new motorcycle for graduation if you got straight "B's." Maybe you are reluctant to go to church because it interrupts your Sunday morning sleep. Yet, should one of your friends try to persuade you that church has no place in modern life, suddenly your religion would take on a stronger, purer image. The list of possible examples is endless. The fact is that we do have images of self, family, friends, and institutions, images that can change in different social settings. Even when only two people are communicating, image is a complex matter, influencing both *what* is said and heard and *how* it is said and heard.

When two people (say your friends Don and Anna) talk to each other, their images of themselves and each other make up a foursome; add the images each thinks the other has of him, and we have a sextet. Add the images each imagines the other holds of himself and we have an octet. Don and Anna may not be conscious of all eight images during the course of the conversation, but their presence nevertheless influences the messages that are sent and the meanings that are assigned to them. The diagram below may clarify this idea for you. The broken line connects the images in Don's head; the unbroken line connects those in Anna's head.

How might this work in a common communication problem? Let's assume you've been appointed to serve on a fund-raising committee to raise enough money for the all-school dance. As you approach various students to put the "bite" on them, you'll have better luck if you view each one as an individual rather than a representative of the entire student body. Instead of rattling off a memorized spiel, you should try to adjust your pitch to fit the personality of each student. If you interpret your audience correctly, adjusting your language and appeal as you go along, you will surely obtain more money for your dance kitty than you would by using a standardized approach. For example, it might be enough to conclude to a close friend, "Joe, we need everybody's help to put this thing over successfully and you can help a lot if between the two of us we set a good example for the others to copy. I'll match whatever you contribute." A complete stranger, on the other hand, someone you reach through the school bulletin, poses more of a problem. He doesn't owe you anything. Therefore, he's less likely to do you any favors. Still, he may be persuaded to chip in for the economic good of all if he benefits in the long run. Your appeal to him might run something like this, once you sized him up:

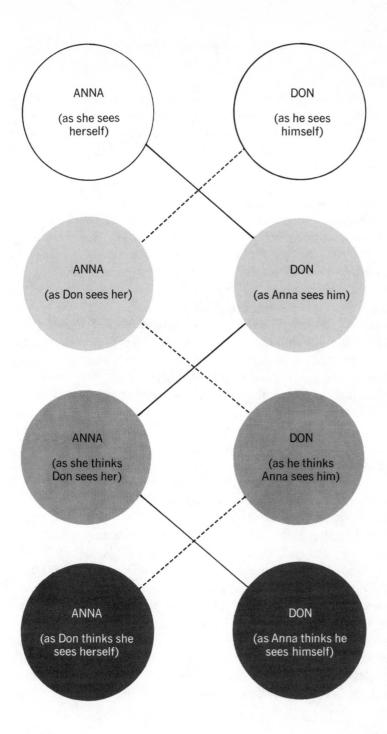

"Wouldn't you rather come to a dance with a live group rather than records? For just a few bucks we'll get to enjoy a really good band."

The stranger poses more of a problem than your close friend because you know nothing about his self-image or his image of you and because you are ignorant, at first, about his value system and the priorities in his life. You could make an on-the-spot evaluation of him to get through to him, but your chances of success will be greatly improved if you spend some time in advance finding an appeal appropriate to him.

People whose livelihood depends upon effective communication have been using this technique of saying the right things to the right people for a long time. Professional speakers use audience analysis so they can fit their approach, level of language, and emphasis to the groups they address. Professional writers use reader profiles. Politicians make great use of pollsters. Advertising specialists depend upon market surveys telling who buys the product and why. Newspaper publishers study their subscribers to find out how old they are, what their education is, what sex they are, how much income they have, and what their political and religious preferences are.

These professional communicators have learned that audience analysis is often a very difficult matter. Generally, the success of their inquiries depends on careful wording of the questions being asked. In a door-to-door survey, for instance, people may be reluctant to state their real opinions in reply to a question about a controversial issue. Or they may give an answer they think is expected of them. For this reason, professional communicators often leave the information gathering to psychologists, sociologists, and other specialists.

Does this mean that you have to be an expert in those fields before you can be a successful communicator? No. While it would be helpful to know something about behavioral psychology, you can do a satisfactory job of gathering information about your receiver(s) by using the concepts of feedback and image. Remember too that your audience is more limited than the professional's. In most cases, the bulk of your communications will be with co-workers, friends, and daily associates. If you think about those people for a minute, you will probably realize that you already know a great deal about them. Being a more successful communicator means building on this information.

Empathy: Stepping into Someone Else's Shoes

A third tool to help you discern your receiver's background and attitudes is empathy—the ability to place yourself in the receiver's shoes. Your purpose in doing this is to try to see yourself, your message, and your objectives from his point of view.

Let's see how this works in a situation where you want to convince someone that the U.S. allots entirely too much money to defense spending. Before you actually begin your pitch you might consider the following: Has your receiver or one of his close relatives been in the military? When—peacetime or wartime? Has he ever been employed in a company that depended on government contracts for producing military goods? Has he traveled outside the U.S. and seen how extensive U.S. military operations are in other countries? What is his attitude toward war—does he think the best defense is good offense, or does he think that carrying a big stick just makes everybody else go out and find one? What are his attitudes toward other areas of the budget that might benefit from reduced defense allocations?

Getting the answers to those questions allows you to approach the receiver in a more effective way. For example, if you know that your receiver fought in World War II and Korea, your argument that the U.S. should stop being the world's big brother would probably fall flat—after all, your receiver spent a good portion of his life fighting to defend that principle. But perhaps your argument that defense spending detracts from other priorities such as urban renewal would be a good one, since your receiver lives in a rundown area of a big city. And maybe your receiver prides himself on his knowledge of psychology; there's an opportunity to stress your theory about big-stick escalation. Using empathy in this way increases your chances of communicating successfully.

Notice too that when we talk of empathy we are not asking you to *accept* the feelings of someone else—that is sympathy.

Empathy only requires you to be *aware* of another's viewpoint: his system of beliefs, his occupations and preoccupations, the things he holds dear, his pet peeves, and so forth. In saying this, however, we do not mean to oversimplify the process of empathizing. In practice, empathy is difficult to achieve even when two individuals are similar in age, interests, political philosophy, and racial, religious, and social backgrounds. When those factors are different, the difficulty increases significantly.

The Dual Roles of Communicators

One last word about this interaction between communicating individuals. We've been talking about them as though we can readily identify one as a sender and one as a receiver. While that distinction makes it easier to explain what happens in communication, the fact is that each of us usually functions as a sender / receiver combined, transmitting ideas and interpreting responses simultaneously. That means that both individuals in a communication situation can make use of these concepts of feedback, image, and empathy.

Summary

This chapter has stressed the importance of feedback, image, and empathy in a good sender-receiver relationship. Feedback makes the communicative process reciprocal. Forming accurate images of yourself and others, and being able to empathize with others, increases the likelihood of a meaningful exchange.

Assignments

1. Summarize the problems and benefits for sender and receiver in the written and the spoken communication situations, in two concisely written paragraphs.

2. Get together with three or four friends. Using a rating scale from one to ten (ten being the best possible score) rate yourself in private on the following personal characteristics: honesty, openness with others, attractiveness, confidence, sensitivity to troubles of others, intelligence. Set this evaluation aside. Then rate each other on the same characteristics, without putting your name on these ratings. Compare your own evaluation of yourself with the way your friends rated you. Discuss the discrepancies between your image of yourself and the images others hold of you.

3. A stranger has asked the way to a certain building. Instead of using traditional directions (street signs, etc.) get him to the building by pointing out specific architectural structures along the way (designate them by appearance rather than by name).

4. Prepare a two-minute oral report on the responsibility of the sender and receiver in the writing situation. Or, prepare a four-minute oral report treating the responsibility of the sender and receiver in the speech situation.

5. Write a set of directions as you did in the third assignment above, but let your destination be some room in your school (starting from the school's main entrance). Assume also that the person to whom you give the directions is blind and cannot speak. He knows how to count and has a white cane. He can read your Braille directions, but he cannot ask help of anyone along the way. In short, direct him by referring to his senses of sound, touch, and smell.

4

Listening

A s YOU MAY HAVE already deduced from the preceding chapters, one of the most important elements in successful spoken communication has nothing to do with speaking. It is the ability to *listen* well that determines whether or not the receiver can accurately decode the sender's message—and, strange though it may seem, it is not an ability that everyone is born with.

Why Study Listening?

You probably aren't exactly convinced that you could benefit from studying listening. After all, you might say, haven't I been listening all my life? And doing all right? We think you can determine your effectiveness as a listener by asking yourself these questions: How long can I remember the things people tell me? How accurately can I remember those things? Most people find that they don't do very well in either respect. Our purpose here will be to show you techniques to improve your listening ability, and therefore your ability to retain and pass on with accuracy information relayed to you. If you conscientiously apply these techniques at home, in school, and on the job, you should become more efficient as student, worker, and personal communicator. Let's see why.

In school and on the job, much information is transmitted in the form of talk. Lectures, discussions, and assignments demand your full attention, comprehension, and recall (listening skills) in the classroom. Lack of skill in any of these three areas results in poor grades. On the job, you'll receive important instructions and directions regarding your duties and responsibilities aurally too. If you fail to comprehend them at the time you receive them, or if you are unable to remember them later, you decrease your usefulness as an employee and may lose the job.

At home, effective listening skills are essential to family harmony and mental health. Inattentive listening on the part of one family member can cause another needless irritation. No one likes to be ignored, especially when they are talking about a matter of great importance to them. A youngster's description of last night's date and a parent's account of an argument with the boss may not be of overwhelming concern to the rest of the family, but should family members fail to pay attention to one another often enough, conversation would become less and less meaningful in that family. Eventually, the effectiveness of inter-family relationships would be reduced. Statements like "I can't seem to talk to my son at all anymore" or "My parents don't understand me" might seem funny to some of us, but they're not humorous in homes where most attempts at communication end in frustration. It's a vicious circle: no family harmony—no listening; no listening—no communication; no communication—no family harmony. However, it need not be that way. Communication works when you work at it. Listening can be productive.

The Listening Process

Remember, listening involves a sender and a receiver. Remember also, for communication between two people to be successful, their relationship must be reciprocal. They must *exchange* feedback with each other in order to appraise the success of their own sending and receiving. The kind of listening we'll describe requires your full attention and 100% involvement as a receiver. We'll ask you to do more than "hear" speakers—we want you to get actively involved with them, their ideas, and the contexts in which you receive and interpret their messages. Why do we stress active involvement? Because it is essential if you hope to come close to understanding another's message. Messages alone are often inadequate means of transferring one person's meaning into another person's head. We need to have an understanding of who the sender is and under what circumstances he sent the message in order to "get" his meaning. The difference in the circumstances under which we receive a message can affect our understanding of the message.

If, for instance, you come out of your front door one spring evening and discover your next-door neighbor sitting on his stoop smoking and exclaiming "What grass!" as he looks out over his front yard, the meaning you derive from that statement will be determined by the man, his message, and the context.

The man

1. His age—if he's over fifty, chances are he's talking about his lawn.

2. His appearance—if he's wearing "straight" clothes, ditto.

3. His reputation—rumor has it he throws wild parties; maybe he doesn't mean lawn at all.

4. Your past observations of him—he goes to work every day; he is clean shaven; he keeps up his property; he must have been referring to his lawn!

The message

1. "What grass"—two simple words, only the second can have two possible meanings: lawn, or marijuana. The word "what" gives no clue; it can apply equally well to either meaning.

The context

In a broad sense, everything in the receiver's span of awareness during the encoding and decoding of a message is part of the context. More specifically, you could be aware of:

1. The man's tone of voice—did he sound sarcastic or proud or disgusted or simply neutral? Any of the four could be used when referring to either lawn or smoke. No help there.

2. His posture—was he slumped over as if disgusted, or serenely relaxed as if contented? Was he furtive or open in his manner? Again, you could read these clues in many ways. Let's keep looking.

3. The lawn—did it look healthy and green and well-trimmed, or was it sickly brown and in need of care? Here you might start matching the condition of the lawn with his posture and tone of voice and reach some conclusions. For example, if the lawn is healthy, his posture is proud, and his voice is contented, the odds are he was talking about his lawn. At the other extreme, if his lawn is a mess, he's slumped over, and he sounds disgusted, he may also mean his lawn. But if he sounds content, he's slumped over, and the lawn's a mess, he may mean his smoke. You can probably see some other possibilities, and we haven't begun to list all the factors that contribute to the context in which you could interpret his meaning.

4. You—what have you been doing lately? How do you feel? What's been on your mind recently? Why does marijuana even come to mind at all? When you heard your neighbor use the word grass, what made you supply the link to marijuana? Was it something you do automatically, or was it something about the way he looked or sounded, or did it have something to do with an article you were just reading in the paper or a story you recently saw on TV? You see, the possibilities as far as the receiver is concerned are numerous. To paraphrase an old saying about beauty, we might say that meaning lies in the mind of the receiver; or, what I think you mean has more to do with my mind than yours.

Let's get back to your neighbor. To narrow down his possible meanings, you need to do some split-second comparing and contrasting of all the information about the man, his message, and the context. You relate some of the physical aspects of the situation (his appearance, the appearance of his lawn, his posture) and some of the psychological aspects (your mental state: happy, sad, frustrated, satisfied; your perception of his mental condition: happy, sad, frustrated, satisfied) to the message itself and you quickly reach some conclusion about what he means: he's talking about his lawn, or he's definitely stoned.

Listening Actively at Home

Listening in the home seems less demanding than listening at school or work, perhaps because you know the senders intimately. You know the extent of their educations, their value systems, their strengths and weaknesses. You have also heard them talk so many times you know their pet themes (Dad's ball games, your brother's "wheels"), their greatest fears (sister Sue's is unresponsive government, Mom's is crime), their favorite times and places for oratory (over the morning paper for Dad, after supper at the dinner table for Mom). Consequently, you can easily predict the conditions that would provoke a speech around your house and what shape the argument is likely to take. It's this predictability that makes listening so easy; you don't have to work hard to understand speeches you've heard before. Or do you? Many times it seems that the very predictability of your parents' remarks is what has caused you to stop listening to them. You may still be *hearing* them, but not *comprehending* them as well as you thought. This is no big deal if all you misunderstood was a set of directions on how to clean out the garage. If you didn't get it straight, you can always ask Mom to repeat it for you. At most, this would represent a minor annoyance for her. But what if her message is more significant than that? What if she is asking you to help out more around the house, to take some of the load off Dad because she is worried about his health? You wouldn't want your half-hearted listening misconstrued as a lack of concern, lest you drive a wedge between you and Mom that would be difficult to remove.

Listening actively may sometimes be nothing more than lending a sympathetic ear to a younger brother or sister's problem and helping them "discover" a solution. A small matter for you, but perhaps a major step in their development.

A second reason listening at home may seem easier is that the context there is familiar—your family's standards, values, goals, and idiosyncrasies. Living so intimately with them all your life, you've developed a continuing frame of reference that enables you to grasp what they mean quickly and readily. When you or someone else in the family leaves for a time, for a vacation or for school, the contexts have to be reestablished. And sometimes new contexts have to be learned. Your brother, for example, back from a summer in Mexico, shares with you a new set of values, experiences, and jargon that now shape the meanings he attaches to words.

You need to be aware that, like predictability of message themes (Dad on the Packers, Mom on crime), familiarity with the context surrounding these themes can also lead to some sloppy listening habits. You may often find yourself thinking you know what a member of your family means just because of the familiar context of his comment, when in fact you haven't bothered to ask to make sure. Feedback in the form of a simple question can often clear up misconceptions readily. For example, your sister Sue is ranting about the indifference of "big government" toward "the common people." Though you have heard her on this topic many times before, you might improve her thinking and your understanding if you ask her to be more explicit: "Sue, which branch or agency or individual in government is indifferent to what needs of what people specifically?" This lets her know you've been listening carefully—more carefully, perhaps, than she's been speaking.

These problems with predictability of theme and familiarity of context are unlikely to arise at school or at work. But different problems make listening well even more challenging in those situations. Let's see why.

Listening Actively at School

Depending upon who is doing the talking, school listening can be almost as comfortable as home listening; or it can be a very difficult task indeed. If an old friend talks about a favorite topic in a mutually understood context, no problem. If a new teacher introduces an unfamiliar concept in a foreign context, no communication. Assuming many listening situations, especially at the start of the term, fit the latter description, what can you do? First, understand what the problem is. The teacher may come from a background that differs from yours. He or she may have a different value system than yours, and therefore a different set of priorities. For example, because they value education and are interested in teaching, teachers may feel their students ought to place a greater emphasis on studying than on finding a good part-time job.

Second, the subject matter is relatively new to you and so is the vocabulary that describes it. How many times have you listened to an explanation of a new concept and just when you thought you knew what the teacher meant, he used a term or phrase that stymied you and the understanding you almost had in your grasp eluded you.

Third, the context of the class lectures and discussions may be strange to you. Some classrooms have a formal air about them which you might mistakenly interpret to mean that no interaction is permissible. In other, more informal classes, you may wrongly conclude that the instructor or the students aren't taking their roles seriously. In either case, you might withhold the kind of feedback the instructor is trying to encourage, and you would both lose. Much of the success of communication is determined by how well we interpret what others expect of us in certain situations, and how well we follow through on that interpretation.

Underlying all of the above problems is the unfamiliarity of the context. The teacher is new, as is the subject, the atmosphere, the ground rules, and the expectations. So much is new that common sense tells us the answer lies in converting the new to the familiar. Let's take teacher, subject, and atmosphere in turn and see how we can accomplish this.

First the teacher. You can break down the barriers surrounding him in the same way you break through to other strangers—interact with him. Ask him questions about his background, his experiences, his expectations of you, and his goals for the course. If you prefer a less direct approach, you can listen for clues or offhand references to the things about him you'd like to know. The first method is faster and involves less speculation (which is always risky), and is the method most instructors prefer. In fact, most instructors answer questions about their course or their qualifications to teach it as a matter of course on the first day.

To better understand your instructor's lectures, nothing is quite as accessible or as comprehensive as a book. Instructors know that many concepts and terms are alien to students, and that is why they assign outside readings to complement the textbook. By reading more authors you will discover different points of view on the same subject, giving you a broader understanding when you discuss concepts in class. While you are reading and studying, the dictionary should be a constant companion to help you handle those new terms you're encountering. Jot down the definitions of the unfamiliar words and review them from time to time so the meanings stay with you. As you study, take notes in your own words that summarize what you have read. Nothing is quite so frustrating as copying a statement directly from a book, only to find later, when you are preparing for a test, that you no longer know what the statement means.

Another useful process is that of "skimming" or previewing a textbook to familiarize yourself with the language, terms, definitions that your instructor will be using in his lectures or discussions. This also prepares you for the contexts surrounding his understanding of the subject.

Guest lecturers may pose a slightly different problem, but you can find out something about them by reading their advance promotional material or by going to the library where you can track them down via *Who's Who,* or the *Reader's Guide to Periodical Literature.* A simpler way to get some inkling (but not always the most reliable information) about the lecturer is from the grapevine. But remember the information you get will be secondhand at least, and therefore of questionable value.

Researching both the speaker and his topic in advance of the speech better equips you to understand the message and provides you with the contexts to help you interpret what he will say. But what can you do to insure that you will be able to accurately remember what he said at a later date? Your ability to recall his message depends on two things: what you do during the talk, and what you do following it.

During the talk you'll want to get as actively involved as possible—with your mind, not your emotions. It is often easy to react so emotionally to what a speaker is saying that you shift the concentration from him to you. When that occurs, you have tuned him out for the time being. Try to suppress any feelings of anger, excitation, joy, or hate; concentrate on *what* he is saying, not on how it makes you feel or how you would "set him straight" if you ever got the chance.

While you're concentrating on the "what" of his message, take brief notes that capture his main ideas. You may want to develop your own system of shorthand to aid you in this. At any rate, take the briefest and clearest notes you can. You'll want them brief so that you won't miss too much of what the speaker says—it's pretty hard to listen while writing lengthy notes. You'll want them clear so that when you go back to them later, they'll make sense to you and require little "doctoring" to be complete.

The best time to jot notes is when the speaker is not talking —when he is shuffling notes, drinking water, clearing his throat, answering a question from the floor. If these opportunities don't present themselves, then write during pauses between major ideas, which he'll identify by saying something like this: "Now that we've seen the impact of violent crime on a national scale, let us turn to the efforts that are being made to combat it in the legislative branch of government." Statements like these are signals to you that the speaker is changing topics or changing the focus of his emphasis, and while you listen with one ear you can quickly jot a summarizing statement in your notebook about his previous main idea. If you miss a point or get confused while trying to write and listen at the same time, don't panic. Leave the note in its incomplete form, devoting your attention to the next idea the speaker is developing. You can always come back to the incomplete note after the lecture.

After the lecture, question your instructor about anything you missed or may have misinterpreted. Or check with other students (pick those whose listening ability you know is better than yours). To be doubly sure you've gotten the intended meaning, you can always clarify what the lecturer said by checking textbooks on the subject. Usually, lecturers will gladly tell you what texts their lectures are based on, or they will steer you toward some books that can provide additional insight into their topic.

At some point after class, you should get in the habit of allowing yourself some "quiet" time to reflect about the lectures or discussions you soaked up that particular day. During this time, you can ponder what was said, how it was said, the kinds of nonverbal signals you picked up that might have influenced your interpretation of what was said. Conversations ("bull sessions") with other students can provide additional interpretations. This kind of sharing is most beneficial as soon after the lecture as possible so that some of the subtle meanings or fine details won't have had time to slip away from your conscious mind.

Lastly, to insure that the vast volume of information you are exposed to in any given semester's lectures and discussions isn't quickly forgotten, set aside some time for weekly review. Go over your notes for every class (be sure to take notes in every class) and get actively involved with them by writing summarizing statements that help you to relate the ideas within each course to each other. You might also try to relate concepts of some of your courses to those that arise in other courses. The relationships between courses like communication skills and psychology are sometimes rather obvious. But with some thought, you may begin to see relationships between courses where you didn't expect them—such as communication skills and data processing, both of which deal with information processing. Once you have learned to relate concepts and see things in larger perspectives, the routine of studying may seem a lot less tiresome.

Listening Actively at Work

Listening at school is aided largely by your active involvement with books and lectures, which forces you to make the new concepts a part of your daily conscious thought and eventually a part of your working knowledge. Listening at work, while just as active, shifts the emphasis of your involvement from books to people.

Adjusting to the strangeness of a new job is complicated by the fact that many people take a "let's wait and see" attitude with you, the new employee. Until they get to know you better, their comments and explanations may be hasty, vague, and abrupt. Little wonder you'll take a strong liking to the person who befriends you the first day on the job. A second problem facing you is learning how the operation works and determining what part you play in it. You realize the need to listen carefully to instructions, interpret them correctly, and then follow through on them, but how can you be assured that you get them right the first time and don't subsequently forget them?

The early information and instructions you receive may puzzle you because you don't know much about either the operation or the jargon used by the other employees. Furthermore, you may know little of the "big picture" (the overall operation of the firm). One of your first concerns should be to determine what the different departments of your firm are, and how each contributes to the business as a whole. The easiest way is to ask questions; if need be, jot down the answers—either on the spot, or later when you have a moment to yourself. Work overtime if possible and come in on weekends and talk to the people around then. They may be more relaxed in the absence of weekday pressures and more willing to answer your questions.

However, doing your job is only part of any working situation; there is also a need to understand and get along with your co-workers and your customers. Good active listening can help here too. Keep your antennae out and you can soon determine your co-workers' attitudes toward each other, their jobs, and their employer. With heightened sensitivity, you can soon determine what they expect of you. You have other sources of information too, such as tone of voice, posture, facial expression, muscle tone, and gestures that always accompany verbal messages and often serve as the only message. If you take the trouble to look beyond the facial expression and the spoken message you may become aware of underlying messages, warning you of mounting tension. Drumming fingers, blinking eyes, frequent wetting of the lips often signal the degree of tension or concentration your associates are feeling. Sometimes an honest compliment or a sincere smile from you can reduce the tension level of both sender and receiver.

Summary

So far in this chapter we have underscored the importance of active involvement with the speaker, the message, and the context(s) if you seek to sharpen your comprehension and retention in a listening situation. We stressed the advantage of familiarizing yourself with the speaker's background, his topic, and the factors that might influence your interpretation of his message. Good listening techniques were recommended for use at home, in school, and on the job. In all three situations you can improve your ability to comprehend a message and retain the content if you make use of the message somehow: in subsequent conversations at home, in analyzing your notes from other courses in school, and in learning about a new process at work. In the concluding section, we add further recommendations for listening problems that are common to the home, school, or work environment.

SUGGESTED SOLUTIONS TO COMMON LISTENING PROBLEMS

QUESTION: How can I listen when what I'm hearing makes me very angry?

ANSWER: Focus on *what* the sender is saying, not on your reaction to it. When you are tempted to interrupt or argue silently, pinch yourself if necessary, then try to summarize his main points so your focus is on him, not you.

QUESTION: How can I listen when I'm so bored I could scream?

ANSWER: If you're really that bored, you had better walk away from the situation. However, if you're only mildly bored (your mind keeps wandering, but you feel no compulsion to scream out loud), try the summary device here too, unless the sender's pace is too fast. If it is, wait until he is through; then summarize.

QUESTION: How can I listen to others when I know the idea I have is so good it ought to be heard first?

ANSWER: Control yourself, listen very carefully and take notes of what those preceding you have to say. They may not say what you expected them to. If it turns out that your ideas really are that superior, you will soon be recognized and eventually may find yourself asked to speak first. If you are never consulted or asked to speak first, you might take another look at your ideas—they may be less outstanding than you think. In any event, keep listening!

QUESTION: What can I do to catch everything a really rapid speaker is saying?

ANSWER: A handy way to cover the "machine gun" style delivery of some speakers is to listen for the *big* ideas they express. Don't get caught up in all the supporting bits and pieces of evidence and opinion; try to capture the main points. If you can mentally outline a speech while you're hearing it, the ideas that you would assign Roman numerals in an outline are the ones you want first. The points you would assign capital letters (A, B, C, etc.) or Arabic numerals (1, 2, 3, etc.) you can always fill in later. Listen for signal phrases like "The biggest single factor in water pollution is . . ." or "If I were asked to identify three foolproof means of foiling the shoplifter, I would say . . ." Phrases like these tip you off that a central idea is coming. Don't forget that after the lecture you can ask others around you to clarify a confusing point, or better yet ask the speaker himself. Lastly, remember that the notes you take are no good to you unless you use them. Review them weekly to keep them "alive" in your memory.

Assignments

1. After a given lecture or discussion, compare your notes with other class members for content and completeness. Try to determine whose short-cut methods are most effective, yours or theirs.

2. Ask your instructor if you can compare your notes with the ones he used to deliver the lecture. Determine your effectiveness.

3. After viewing or hearing a news commentator, compare what you thought you heard with what other family members listening with you thought they heard. Try to determine which words or phrases may have led to different interpretations.

4. Watch a 1940s war movie on TV and note the patriotic appeals used. Write a short paper explaining what effect the appeals had on you and why. Ask your parents and grandparents what effect they had in the 1940s.

5. Observe guests on the late-night talk shows for signs of nervousness or self-assurance. In class next day, discuss and compare what you noticed with your classmates. Note particularly what verbal, vocal, bodily, or muscular signal tipped you off.

5
Reading

JUST AS OUR ABILITY to listen affects our understanding of a spoken communication, so does the way we read influence our understanding of a written message. In this chapter, we deal with the act of reading as a crucial element in the communication process.

At some time you may have seen advertised, in your local paper or on TV, special reading programs that guarantee to increase your reading speed by thousands of words per minute and your comprehension by fifty to seventy-five percent. While we wish we could offer such miraculous results in one chapter on reading, we have to say frankly that what we are trying to do is much more limited: to suggest how your reading can be made more efficient. Hopefully, following our suggestions will not involve any massive overhaul of the way you've been reading, and it certainly won't commit you to sitting by a reading pacer machine for hours on end. We ask you to think of reading in terms of communication, focusing on two readers, Gene and Lou, as they read various materials during a typical day. Then we draw some conclusions about those two individuals as receivers.

We begin with a basic point: reading is one half of an act of communication. You, the reader, are receiving ideas, information, and impressions in the form of a message from a sender, a writer. As in listening, your success in receiving that message depends on how actively involved you can become, in this case with the reading materials in front of you.

This means that reading is not just taking in print with your eyes. Rather, it is your responding to thoughts, data, and different kinds of reading matter in such a way that you can get out of the message whatever you need to get. Good reading, like good listening, requires desire and interest on your part. It also demands a variety of approaches.

To illustrate these points let's look at two readers, Gene and Lou, as they go through a typical day. In advance, we'll identify Gene as a poor reader and Lou as a good one.

A Passive Reader

Gene is nineteen, a part-time student in a community college and a part-time mechanic. His day begins with a quick breakfast after which he's off to classes at his school. Once at school his reading activity begins, for his first two hours at school are spent preparing for his classes in psychology, math, and automotive engine design.

Gene reads these psych, math, and auto engine texts in the same way. He goes to the assigned chapter, reads straight through, skims over definitions he is not sure of (assuming they'll be clearer later), reads all sections at the same speed (rather slowly), doesn't take notes, and doesn't go back when finished with the chapter. After his reading is finished, he goes to class, thinking that he has done the assigned work. "I put in as much time reading as the next guy," he thinks. "I've done my job."

Later in the day, after his classes, Gene goes to work at a local garage where he is a part-time mechanic. Today he's been assigned to do a brake job on a foreign car, a model he's never worked on before. Luckily, the owner has provided Gene with a shop manual for the car, and Gene is glad to have it. It will help him out, he thinks.

Gene starts going through the brake job procedure as outlined in the manual. There are fourteen steps, and he follows the order step by step. However, when he gets down to step number eight he discovers that he made a mistake in step number five—he inserted a pin-shaft the wrong way. Angry at the book for not alerting him to the potential problem, he redoes steps five through eight and then finishes the remaining procedure. He writes up the billing order, tosses the shop manual into the front seat of the car, and thinks to himself: "Somebody ought to learn how to write How-To books so that mechanics can't foul up." (Gene never saw an illustration which would have prevented his goof.)

Work ends at half-past six. Gene goes home to dinner, after which he reads the evening newspaper. He starts by covering most articles on the front pages, reads most of the editorial pages, then finishes with the sports pages. He reads the news stories all the way through from start to finish, accepting the information as fact; he reads the editorials as though they were news stories. It takes him a good hour and a half, sometimes, to get through the paper, which often leaves him too tired to tackle other reading material that interests him. (Tonight is one of those nights when he feels frustrated; he had bought a copy of *Car and Driver* today, hoping to read it before bed, but he's just too exhausted.)

As we have said, Gene is a poor reader. Let's explore the reasons for his reading problems.

First of all, Gene reads without any direction. He seldom if ever identifies *why* he is reading something. True, he knows in the back of his mind that he has to read textbooks to get through school. He knows too that he needs to read the shop manual in order to get the brake job right on the foreign car. And he knows that a newspaper will keep him up to date on the news. But he never tries to find more specific reasons. He never stops to think that there might be a special way of reading an auto engine design textbook because of a special interest he has in the subject. It has never dawned on him that he might read a psychology text in a different way because the nature of the material is different. Nor does he realize that a person might read a newspaper with a more concrete purpose than just keeping up to date on the news.

Second, Gene reads all these materials as if they were written the same way. Newspaper, psychology text, shop manual— to Gene, in every case the writer is simply offering information at random, stopping whenever he thinks he's covered the ground. That may explain why Gene reads every word and every paragraph. After all, according to his thinking, if writers (senders) just toss words out at random, then you never know when you might come across something important. Therefore it's pretty important to catch every last noun, verb, adjective, or adverb.

Perhaps that explains in turn why Gene reads everything only once. If he covers every word, he thinks, then he can't possibly have missed any point the first time through. So why go back a second time?

That same reason may account for Gene's reading without the aid of a pencil to take notes. Gene may think he is comprehending more than he actually is. (His tests at school will probably show otherwise.)

Whatever the reasons for Gene's steamroller approach to reading, the philosophy behind it is best summed up in his own words, "I put in as much time reading as the next guy. I've done my job." To Gene, efficient reading is a matter of the number of hours or minutes he puts in. For him reading is a passive operation, the mechanical absorption of ideas, the comprehension of a message by some mysterious process of osmosis. He equates understanding with a certain amount of elapsed time; he is not so much a receiver as a mental receptacle, and a rusty one at that.

An Active Reader

We turn now to Lou, who makes far better use of his reading time. Like Gene, Lou is almost twenty and a part-time student and employee. His reading day takes in many of the same materials Gene's did.

Lou's day begins with a brief study session too, before his classes at his community college—the same ones Gene is in. But if Gene and Lou are similar in setting aside this time for study, they certainly use it very differently. For one thing, when Lou takes up his psychology textbook he doesn't start with the chapter assigned for the day. Rather, he begins with a two-minute review of the previous chapter, touching on the main headings, rereading key definitions and the concluding points. In this way Lou reestablishes the context for the chapter he is about to read, ensuring the continuity of the writer's message.

Then he turns to the assigned chapter. He scans the chapter introduction, if any, leafs through to find out what the subheadings are, glances quickly at any illustrations, graphs, etc. to find out their focus, goes to the end of the chapter where he reads any summaries, then looks at the review questions and assignments at the very end.

All this takes roughly five to ten minutes. While Lou is doing this, he is carrying on a mental dialogue with himself. "Why is this chapter organized around those three points about psychological conditioning? How does the chart on page 72 fit in with the subheading under which the material is included? Which of the review questions at the end of the chapter would my instructor be inclined to ask on a test? What does the term 'Gestalt psychology' mean?"

Then Lou asks himself three key questions: "What do I expect to gain from this material? What does the author want me to get from this? How should I read this text in comparison to others?"

After determining his purpose in reading the chapter, and the best way to approach it, he begins going through the text. He reads the material rather rapidly to get the central ideas; then he goes back, spending time on definitions, jotting notes in the margin (thereby translating the material into his own language), numbering certain points where the text breaks down an idea into several parts (see Figure 3 for an example). He varies his pace according to the difficulty of the material and his instructor's predictable emphasis on some sections. When he gets to the end of the chapter he closes his eyes a minute, summarizes what he thinks were the main points, verifies his summary with any summary in the text itself, and then answers the review questions, going back into the chapter as necessary to find a precise answer.

Lou varies his approach for other texts. In the case of math texts, he does the same preliminary work as he did with the psychology text—previewing and scanning the material—but he spends less time on this step. He knows that going through mathematical material demands careful, word-by-word reading in most cases, since a person cannot understand a second point until he grasps the first one. In other words, reading a psychology textbook is a bit like working a picture puzzle. To a degree you can get the full picture by putting together separate pieces. But mathematics involves stringing together a connected series of items, grasping a sequence of steps in order to understand the overall message. It's more like working a maze—you can't get to point Y without getting to point X first. So Lou reads more slowly and carefully, making sure he understands key points before going on.

In many cases this involves memorizing formulas and equation patterns. Lou either stops at times in his reading to do this memory work, or he notes that he will have to come back later and do it. Either way he can further test his understanding of the message when he finishes his reading by doing one or two review problems.

Lou also reads the same automotive engine design book Gene reads. Lou's method here is to preview the chapter first, looking for its overall concepts, relating the chapter's emphasis to what he thinks his own and his instructor's emphasis is.

After previewing he reads the chapter, dividing his attention between the words and illustrations. He knows that texts in his technical field usually explain a lot of points by diagrams, photographs, and the like, so he is always alert to any illustrations. He reads three or four paragraphs, goes back to an illustration to make sure he can visualize the concept or process described, and then moves on to the next point. He varies his reading speed according to the difficulty of the material, and, again, his instructor's predictable interest or lack of interest in the specific subjects. At the end of the chapter he does the review questions, if any, to check his comprehension.

As is pretty obvious by now, Lou is a highly active—therefore efficient—reader. Further evidence of this ability appears if we watch him reading other materials at work and at home.

Since he works as a shipping clerk in a mail-order company, his reading there consists mainly of letters people have sent to the company. These contain information as to which goods Lou should send out. Lou approaches these as most good readers in the business world do, by looking for an overall unifying point in the first paragraph and for specific information in those that follow. Lou knows that written business communications are generally organized in this way.

Psychological Environments

might be inclined to overlook environmental influences on behavior. Doing so ignores a basic premise of psychology—that all *living mechanisms are conditioned by factors in their surroundings*. *Key point in chapter-summary*

This has been shown in experiments on rats. To take one example, researchers have shown convincingly that behavior of rats changes as more and more rats are put into a fixed area, limiting their space individually. Jones and Symon found that as rat population increased, three changes in behavior took place. *rat example as proof*

First, rats became more aggressive—more inclined to bite one another and vie for territory. Second, the rats grew less and less able to control motor functioning—they became more twitchy and less coordinated. Third, they took longer to wake after sleeping. In the increasingly overpopulated rat populations time for reaching a "waked state" was prolonged.

We're controlled by things outside us.

3 changes in rat behavior:
1. aggression
2. twitchiness
3. waking time

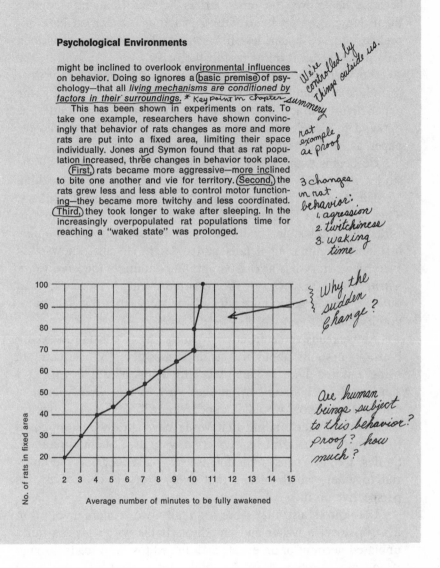

Why the sudden change?

Are human beings subject to this behavior? proof? how much?

Figure 3.   A Sample of Lou's Note-taking

He does two other things in reading these business letters: he looks for lists, and checks off with a pencil items he has gotten from stock and boxed for the customer. He looks for lists because he knows the order letters he gets frequently contain them. He checks off items with a pencil as a check on his comprehension; he's much less likely to duplicate or forget a stock item if he checks it off as he fills the order.

Work ends for Lou at approximately the same time it does for Gene, around half-past six, leaving time for reading the paper *before* dinner. This takes Lou about forty-five minutes, as opposed to Gene's hour and a half *after* dinner. Lou tackles the paper as he does other reading material—with a plan.

He begins with the front news pages. He doesn't read all the stories there, only the ones that will be of real interest to him. Neither does he read every paragraph of every story he selects. That is because he knows that news stories are written in "inverted pyramid style," with the most newsworthy facts coming first and illuminating details added later. He also knows that every news story has a *lead* paragraph containing the *who, what, when, where,* and *why* of the reported event. If he has to read quickly, he can get a quick idea of the story from this lead paragraph alone.

As he reads these front-page stories he is constantly asking himself questions about the sender's message: "What facts are being ignored here? What facts are being played down? If I were reading this story in another part of the country or in a different city, how would it appear there?" These questions reflect Lou's understanding that while news stories are supposed to be factual, the term *fact* covers a wide area of interpretation. Stories, too, don't just write themselves—a sender puts the material together, which means that every story is colored by his perspective on it.

Lou knows also that there are really two senders involved in a news story: a writer and an editor. If the writer gives a fairly unbiased account of an event, then the editor, who reads through it and makes any changes he thinks are needed, may not be so fair (or vice versa). Lou determines the extent of this "editorial slanting" by checking out several points. First he notes where the story has been placed. Editors, he knows, like to play up their favorite causes and philosophies near the top of the page, up in the big headlines if possible. Thus, an editor who favors no-fault insurance may put a favorable story about that subject right up there in big print, while an editor who opposes it will put the story down at the bottom of the front page or back on page three. Similarly, a Democratic editor who finds a story that puts a Republican in a bad light will headline that item, while "burying" inside the paper an article that's unfavorable to the Democrats.

Next, Lou checks the proportion of space devoted to each story—how many inches of print are allotted to various issues, events, and personalities. Length of story is another index of an editor's concern about a particular subject. And he checks to see what items are placed next to one another—frequently an editor can play down the importance of one story by placing some trivial or ludicrous item alongside it. For example, Lou remembers seeing a recent article about his U.S. senator. Next to it, a hostile editor had placed a story about a hippopotamus at the Washington Zoo.

Lou moves on to the editorial page after the news pages. He knows the editorials are meant to give the opinions of those who write them, so he reads these differently than the news stories. First, he ascertains the main idea behind each editorial. Then he applies the following tests:

1. How much evidence is there for what the editorialist says? One or two examples do not make a convincing case.

2. Are the examples glaring exceptions or more typical instances? One sensational case of heroin addiction doesn't mean a whole city is being overrun with heroin traffic. One vivid budget-cutting move by the federal government doesn't lead to economic salvation for everyone.

3. If statistics are used, how reliable is the sample on which they are based? A poll of 100 people isn't half as solid as one based on 10,000.

4. Are the statistics calculated in relation to all relevant factors or treated in isolation? A reported twenty percent rise in crime for an area, for example, isn't valid unless that number is looked at in comparison to growth of population for the same area.

5. How is the argument structured? Frequently an editorial sounds convincing just because the writer organized his ideas so that the reader is left with only two limited choices—total gun control or none at all—when the real answer to the problem may lie between those two extremes, or entirely outside of them.

Lou comes away from the editorials better informed. He has been alert to the weaknesses as well as the strengths of the sender's arguments. He realizes that few of the controversial problems treated in editorials can be resolved as easily as editorial writers would have him believe.

Lou isn't half so wary, naturally, when he's reading the sports pages, which he does for pleasure. These he covers at a leisurely pace, savoring the interesting sections of feature stories, spending some time rereading well-phrased passages, reviewing dramatic or amusing incidents. In the back of his mind he thinks, "I've done the hard work of reading by now. I can afford to enjoy this material more for its own sake. I'll amble through it and spend time on the great descriptions that columnist usually writes. But I won't overdo it—I want to be able to enjoy those three articles I spotted in my latest issue of *Hi-Fi Stereo Review*. I want to read those tonight, before bed."

These articles in Lou's hobby magazines, his last reading of the day, tend to be essays, and Lou reads them in one of two ways. If he thinks the article is important, he reads it straight through quickly and goes back more slowly a second time. If he thinks it does not offer information he particularly needs, he may start by reading the first couple of paragraphs, skip to the final paragraphs, and then go back to the middle, reading just the topic sentence of each paragraph there. Lou uses the first method when he wants to remember specific points made in the article, the second when he is looking for an overall summary.

He knows the second method is a useful one because writers of essays use a familiar organization pattern. The opening paragraphs indicate the direction of the material, the body of the article gives the evidence, and the end presents the writer's conclusions. If Lou isn't too concerned about the evidence, he can skip right to the conclusion from the opening paragraphs—that gets him a quick summary without the work of reading everything.

As we have said earlier, Lou is an excellent reader. Let's explain what he's doing right, just as we explained Gene's mistakes.

First of all Lou finds a concrete reason for reading before he actually begins doing so. He focuses the reading on a task he has to accomplish, or a personal interest he has in the material. Notice that he asked himself "What do I expect to gain from this material?" before he started his morning study session with his textbooks. Notice also that he read only certain news stories, and that he had preselected three articles from the hobby magazine he read before bed.

Second, Lou previews material before reading it. He skims the subheadings, chapter outlines, summaries, and review questions in textbooks. He asks questions about the possible biases in a news story. He tries to predict what the argument will be in an editorial. In every case he thinks about the content in advance. Thus he is more likely to be receptive to the message.

Third, Lou adjusts his overall approach according to the kind of reading matter he is dealing with. Math texts are read differently than psychology texts, which are read differently than newspapers or magazines, which are read differently than letters. Lou knows that writers don't just spout information at random—they organize material according to patterns that will make it easy for the reader to understand their message. As a receiver, Lou selects a reading method to conform to the pattern of a particular piece of writing.

Fourth, Lou adjusts his technique as he goes along, according to his purpose. He stops for hard formulas, for example, in textbooks. He takes advantage of lists in order letters by checking off the items on the lists. In the middle of a news story he'll check where the story is placed in the paper—next to what? In the middle of an editorial he'll stop and ask if the example used as proof is more dramatic than typical (therefore not valid as evidence). He is constantly alert to ways in which he can better relate to the message, sometimes agreeing with it, as many times not.

Fifth, Lou varies his reading pace. The math text requires slower reading than his psychology or engine design texts. The letters at work require deliberate scrutiny. But some news stories aren't so important in his eyes, so he can go faster. And he can skim the articles that don't really interest him, in his *Hi-Fi Stereo Review*—he can race along in those if he wants to.

Sixth, he reviews periodically. Notice that before he started a new chapter in his textbooks, he went back over material in previous chapters. Lou knows that short review periods like this, accompanied by longer review sessions before tests, allow him to remember and understand more than if he put in one long "cram session" the night before an exam. The reasons? Shorter, periodic review increases his ability to remember, and he can keep the continuity of learning more coherent.

Seventh and last, Lou frequently uses marginal notations and other markings to increase his comprehension of key ideas (see Figure 3, p. 51). He knows that his understanding of the material improves when he puts the material in his own words or otherwise highlights important phrases, organizational numberings, and the like. Such markings allow him to digest the material, making it his own. In addition, they permit him to review at test time rather than reread everything.

The Rewards of Active Reading

All these characteristics of Lou's reading point back to our initial emphasis in this chapter: a good reader is one who involves himself actively with the message and the sender in relation to his own purposes in reading. Lou is a good reader because he sees reading as an act of participation in the message and a lively response to the different kinds of printed matter. Unlike Gene, who concluded that putting in so many hours of time was doing the job of reading, Lou measures his efficiency by how much he gets out of the material minute by minute.

We raise this point about time to make a concluding point. Being a good reader doesn't really take any more time than being a poor one—Lou covered more ground than Gene did, in the same amount of time. It does involve more work on a second-by-second and minute-by-minute basis, however.

Where does this leave you? It means that if you want to become a good reader, you'll have to stay more alert as you move along through those sentences and paragraphs. But the reward for that is being able to comprehend and evaluate a sender's message better. We think that means you'll be able to achieve more, and enjoy it at the same time, which is well worth the price of a more concentrated effort.

Summary

Reading should be an active response to a message. Passive readers read without any direction, read all materials in the same way, read every word, and read materials only once. They measure efficient reading by how many hours they put into it. Active readers have a concrete reason for reading, preview material before getting into it, adjust their overall approaches according to the kind of material, adjust their approaches as they go along according to their purpose, vary their pace, review periodically, and use marginal notation frequently. They put in no more time than poor readers; they merely use their time more wisely.

Assignments

1. Write two or three paragraphs explaining some good methods for reading this chapter.

2. Participate in a discussion group before your class, in which you explain briefly how this or another textbook is organized.

3. In a one-page essay explain the best way to read *one* of the following items: a poem, a short story, a novel, a play, a biography, a detective story.

4. Bring to class the front section of your local paper. Using it as a visual aid, explain in a five-minute talk what the paper's biases are. Point out to your classmates the placement of articles and proportions of space devoted to certain subjects.

5. Clip an editorial from a newspaper. Using the same tests Lou applied in this chapter, decide how valid the central point is. Then write a one- or two-paragraph evaluation for your instructor. Don't forget to give him the article with your evaluation.

6. Try Lou's second method of reading a magazine article— reading the opening paragraphs first, skipping to the final ones, and then skimming the topic sentences of the middle ones. How useful do you find the method? Share your experience in a small-group discussion with four others who also tried the technique.

6

The Informative Message in Spoken Communication

THUS FAR, WE HAVE stressed the role of the receiver in successful communication, describing various techniques for listening and reading as effectively as possible. At this point we turn to the role of the sender, shifting our emphasis from the understanding of a message to the formulation of that message. We begin in this chapter by discussing the informative spoken message, from the conception of the idea to the final speech, and proceed in later chapters to other kinds of communications.

Before going further, it may be worthwhile to examine what is meant by the term "informative message," in order to head off any misunderstandings or confusion that may arise later.

Traditionally, speeches have been grouped into two general categories: informative and persuasive. These designations are based not on the content of the speech, but rather on the intent of the speaker. For example, a speech explaining how a bill gets introduced and passed in the legislature would be informative; if the same speech was intended to convince you that a particular bill should be passed, then it would be persuasive.

Obviously, each of the above speech types could include elements of the other. The informative speech often does contain persuasion, if the speaker must convince his audience that the information is important to them. Even a situation as seemingly nonpersuasive as a speech explaining company procedure for answering letters of inquiry can contain persuasive elements, as the speaker might occasionally editorialize about the "company" way being the best way.

We can readily see that a speech to persuade must contain some informative elements, because before you can urge the acceptance of an idea, you must first explain the idea. Even supposedly purely informative speeches can be persuasive if the speaker wants the audience to draw a particular conclusion. When in doubt, consider the *intent*, not the *content*, of the message to determine its classification.

Why Study Spoken Communication?

It's probably hard for you to think of spoken communication as something you need to *learn*. After all, you've been talking all your life. Ask yourself one question, though: how good are you at holding the attention of your audience? If, like most of us, you don't think your listeners are as impressed as they might be, perhaps there is something you can do about it. Even if you never have to give a formal speech before a large group, you are in a sense addressing an "audience" whenever you try to communicate something to one or two individuals in a casual conversation; and the techniques of speech preparation and delivery we shall discuss here are applicable to *any* act of spoken communication. We all spend a lot of time talking with others, and the more skilled we are at communicating with our friends and co-workers, the more likely we are to achieve our business and social goals and the greater will be our personal satisfaction.

Purpose: The Intent of the Message

Successful spoken communication, like successful written communication, is rarely an accident. It begins with a purpose, and is organized to express that purpose and bring about the desired listener response. A dull, rambling speaker is no fun to listen to, and is likely to "lose" his audience. Because he doesn't know where he is going, his listeners won't either. Failure to define purpose clearly is the most common cause of unsuccessful communication, written or spoken. The better you understand your own purpose, the better your listener will understand it.

It is useful to distinguish between two purposes: the general purpose of the speech, which might be to inform or persuade; and the specific purpose—the precise message you wish to communicate to your listeners. For example, if your teacher asks each of you to present a brief report in class on any subject you wish, you will all be concerned with the general goal of informing an audience. But each of you will have a different specific message to convey, depending on the topic you happen to choose. Tom might want to explain the five steps he follows when buying a used car. Sue might want to describe the basic strumming and fingering positions for playing a simple tune on a guitar. Bill might set forth the merits and flaws of several types of cameras that might be used by an amateur photographer, all in the same price range.

Each of these reports will be quite different from the others, not only because the topics are different but because each speaker has *limited* his topic to a very specific idea. Why is this so important? Suppose Tom decided to tell his audience "something about" purchasing a used car. He might have some very valuable, tried-and-true ideas on the subject, but he would probably express them in a vague and disorganized manner, and chances are his audience would end up just as likely to purchase a lemon as they were before he started. How can Tom make his purpose as precise as possible?

Let's assume he has been given a five-minute time limit. Probably, he will want to allow about half a minute to a minute for the introduction and another half-minute for the concluding remarks, leaving about three and one-half to four minutes for the body—the important information he wants to communicate. Four minutes may sound like a long time, but if he knows his subject well enough he'll have so much to say that the four minutes will shrink alarmingly. There's a solution, however: he can plan ahead. Sorting and evaluating his information before he puts it together in a talk will help Tom narrow down his purpose, which in turn will ensure for him the kind of audience response he's after. He hopes his listeners will (a) recognize the importance of his message; and (b) relate the units of information he is passing along, so his message will be of some future use to them.

He begins by sitting down with pencil and paper and considering several factors: his knowledge of the topic; his audience's knowledge of and attitudes toward the topic; the occasion; the setting (physical surroundings and general atmosphere) of his talk; and the time limit. As we noted in chapter 3, these variables are present in any spoken communication situation. If we are conversing informally, we take them into account almost subconsciously, while the conversation is in progress. But in a more formal situation, we need to think about them in advance, and adjust our speech accordingly.

For Tom, several of those factors are easy to define, such as time limit, occasion, physical setting, and his knowledge of the subject. But the others—his audience's knowledge and attitudes, the prevailing atmosphere in the classroom at the time he speaks —are harder to predict. Hopefully, by using some common sense, questioning his classmates carefully, and observing them discreetly, he will have a better understanding of these factors by the time his turn comes to speak.

DETERMINING AUDIENCE KNOWLEDGE AND ATTITUDES

Tom knows his classmates are much like him in terms of general knowledge and interests, as well as age, socioeconomic level, and prior schooling. Mainly, they will differ in personal experiences and special interests, some of which may affect their ideas on the subject Tom plans to discuss. Just what these ideas are Tom can best discover by simply asking some of them a few general questions about cars, to determine their overall background in the subject; and, more specifically, by asking how they feel about buying a used car as opposed to a new model. Their answers will not only enable him to omit from his speech whatever information his classmates already have (and include those points that are new to them); they will also provide him with a better picture of what his classmates want to know.

After talking with his friends, Tom has established in his mind a rough "audience profile." He has learned that his audience's knowledge of used cars is quite general, with the possible exception of a few classmates whose hobby is drag racing. He'll have to make some comments in the course of his speech to indicate that he is aware of their advanced knowledge, but he must fill in the gaps for the others who are less expert in the subject. At the same time, he must be completely honest with himself about his *own* background. He would risk a serious loss of face should he attempt to talk knowledgeably about a subject he had not explored thoroughly.

Let's assume that Tom has jotted down the following brief list (four to five points for a speech this short) of what he considers important things to check in a used car.

1. engine
2. transmission
3. body
4. brakes
5. tires

He knows that any of these items can be the source of expensive repairs if they are in poor condition. However, he's not too sure what a nonmechanic might do to ascertain whether or not these parts are in good working order. At this point he decides to make up two lists which he knows will save him a lot of time, frustration, and embarrassment. One list is headed "The things I know about this subject," and the other "The things I don't know about this subject."

This preliminary questioning forces Tom to level with himself. In addition, it provides him with a greater insight into the topic. If he's really being candid, his "don't-know" list will tend to be a good deal longer than his "do-know" list, and this is quite normal. His initial reaction to the longer "don't-know" list might be to chuck the whole idea and choose another topic. Sometimes this is the wisest course of action. But there is one strong argument for staying with his original topic: he probably chose it in the first place because of this strong interest in it. If that is the case, his next step will be some preliminary digging in the library to see if he can readily fill in the gaps on his "don't-know" list. Half an hour with the *Reader's Guide to Periodical Literature* will be far more productive than time spent thumbing through auto-oriented magazines on the rack. By skimming the many articles the *Guide* directs him to, he can get a good indication of all that's involved in selecting a used car and some pointers on how his audience might check out the various parts. If he still feels ill-at-ease with the topic, if it just doesn't seem to "fit" him, then he should scrap it and follow the course of action outlined above with a new idea.

EVALUATING THE INFORMATION

Assuming Tom elects to stick with used-car buying, he should now read through his source material again, more carefully, to answer the questions on his "don't-know" list. A second session with the list, adding new information as well as new questions raised by his reading, will improve his understanding of his subject. And finally, after another reading session, he is ready to *sort out* his information according to the same criteria he used when selecting a topic. Questions he might keep foremost in his mind are: what does my audience really need to know about this subject? how much can I present fully in four minutes (as opposed to squeezing into five minutes)? what things will I have to omit because it would take up too much time to explain them? and lastly, what bits of data have I come across that can make this topic come alive and make them want to listen? Sorting through the facts in this fashion will help Tom start to see his subject through his audience's eyes. Later, when he is in the process of organizing the material, he should attempt to hear his explanations through the ears of his audience.

This process of sorting and evaluating should enable Tom to begin to formulate a specific purpose that is brief and to the point. His original list of five items to check when appraising a used car may have grown as he looked over the articles he discovered in the library. It may now include such things as rust spots, wiring, exhaust system, alignment of frame, mileage, condition of interior, and so on. In addition, he may have considered emphasizing other ways of approaching a used-car purchase. As he read, he probably discovered preliminary actions the prospective buyer might take that could save him time before going to the car lot. For example, he might check to see how much he could borrow from the different lending institutions if he did not have the cash on hand; at the same time he could compare interest rates and charges. He might want to check the state insurance laws to see how much insurance he will need, and call an insurance company to learn what it will cost. Also, he might decide in advance exactly what kind of car he really needs and what kind of car he can afford.

Tom realizes that any one of these topics could make a separate four-minute speech by itself. If he wants to stick with the original subject of how to appraise a used car, he will have to weigh his initial list against the new additions he came up with. He'll have to decide which points are most relevant and most interesting, which he can speak most knowledgeably about, and which can be adequately covered in the allotted time. The weeding-out technique will probably reduce the list to no more than two or three items. For example, any of the five original points (engine, transmission, body, brakes, tires), if covered in depth, could take much more than four minutes. Tom might want to consider only those checks applied to the car as it stood motionless with the motor off, such as rusting, body, tires, interior. Or he might want to discuss only those involved in a road test such as engine, transmission, brakes, front end. Whatever he ultimately singles out to include in his presentation is determined by the factors of relevancy, clarity, interest, his own knowledge, and time limitations.

Let's assume finally that he elects to cover the items that can be checked when the car is standing still in the car lot—rusting, body, tires, mileage, and upholstery. This would probably be a wise choice because it will be relatively easy to make the discussion clear and interesting to those who have almost no previous knowledge about cars. At the same time, the information he provides will be specific enough so there is a good chance that even the drag-racers may learn something—few people know everything about even their favorite topic. A more technical discussion of engine diagnoses might guarantee the attention of car enthusiasts but could also guarantee losing the rest of his audience completely.

Perhaps, as you have been following the development of Tom's topic, some purpose statements may have already occurred to you; you may want to jot them down now so that you will have a better perspective of Tom's problem later. Here are a few purpose statements Tom might come up with.

1. How to buy a used car.

2. Things to look for when buying a used car.

3. How to appraise a used car after normal business hours.

4. Five simple tests to apply to a used car before you road test it.

5. Five obvious clues to the condition of a used car that can save the potential buyer time and money.

Obviously, Tom is becoming more specific and precise with each effort he makes to designate the purpose of his message. The first three he would discard out of hand because they are much too vague and general. While the third indicates a potentially interesting tack, it is still far too broad. The last two narrow the scope considerably because they qualify or limit what is to be covered, while also describing the subject to be discussed. Armed with this type of purpose statement, Tom's decisions on how to organize his information are greatly simplified. If he had stopped with his first statement of purpose, the job of organizing would be much more difficult, and the burden of clarification would be greater for both speaker and audience.

Organizing the Body of the Speech

It is very probable that while sorting and evaluating the data he accumulated, Tom came up with some ideas on how to approach the topic he was seeking to limit and clarify. This approach or "angle" is fundamental to the effective organization of an informative message. Tom's last three statements of purpose suggest that the matter of organization had already been considered; this simultaneous analysis of purpose and structure is one of the beneficial by-products of researching a topic and allowing time for reflective thinking afterwards. The question facing Tom now is, which of the various methods of organization he has considered will best suit his purpose? He knows the structure of his talk should be a natural outgrowth of the data, not an arbitrary arrangement imposed upon the subject. Rather than thinking, "Well, I haven't tried a chronological organization or problem-solving approach in previous talks, so perhaps I should use one of those methods now," he refers to his data and the nature of his topic, aware that his specific purpose will suggest which method is best for this particular talk. We provide the list of organizational patterns or methods that follows merely to acquaint you with some of the possible choices. You have undoubtedly already used many without knowing there were names for them.

1. *Chronological order.* Here you describe a series of events or explain how to perform a process, discussing the various happenings or steps involved in the order in which they naturally occur—from first to last. You might analyze the events leading up to the Battle of Gettysburg, or tell how to develop a roll of film. In some cases, you might want to use reverse chronological order, especially in combination with another of the techniques, such as cause-effect.

2. *Spatial sequence.* This technique is ideal for topics that fall naturally into a spatial context. For example, a weather system flowing from the West Coast to the East Coast of the U.S. would be organized to cover the system's progress across the country. Also used for explanations of the workings of machinery like watches, rockets, engines, etc.

3. *Problem-solving.* A handy method for the persuasive speech, but also useful in the informative talk if used with discretion. The speaker first defines the problem and then offers solutions. (In an informative talk the speaker would proceed impartially, i.e., examining all possible solutions as objectively as possible.)

4. *Cause-effect.* By first describing certain events and then tracing their effects, a speaker can give his audience a useful perspective on a historical occurrence; also good for explaining scientific developments or theories. This method is often combined with others, e.g., chronological and problem-solving. Often used in reverse for special effect.

5. *Topical sequence.* A method of classifying or categorizing data (as in a topical outline), useful for explanations of organization of governments, solar systems, etc.

6. *Familiar-to-unfamiliar (comparison).* Here you use something

familiar to explain the unfamiliar, ideal for the informative speech and the persuasive as well. For example, you might compare the speed of a camera shutter (unfamiliar) to the blink of an eyelid (familiar).

7. *Familiar-to-unfamiliar (contrast)*. Here again the familiar is used to explain the unfamiliar, but the two things are different rather than alike: "Manfield University is so large today that most freshman lectures will have as many as 300 students in the audience. But when Manfield was founded 100 years ago, the entire student body would not have filled one half of that lecture hall." Frequently, comparison and contrast are paired for effect.

8. *Climax-anticlimax*. Simply put: either build to a climax or begin with your strongest point. The climax is more common in the persuasive effort; the anticlimax is typical of the informative presentation.

The above list is not an exhaustive treatment of the patterns of organizational development, but rather a summary of some commonly used methods. Tom would probably find that his material lent itself best to a chronological, spatial, problem-solving, or topical approach. Less useful, for Tom, would be the cause-effect or climax arrangements. Assuming he has selected one of the appropriate methods of arrangement, let us see how he might organize the entire speech.

Organization of the Whole Speech

Traditionally, speech authorities have recognized that a unified message has at least three parts: the introduction, the body, and the conclusion. You are more likely to be understood if you introduce the main body of your message with an explanation of *why* your subject is of concern to your audience; *how much* you intend to say about that subject; and *what* you expect them to do with the information when you are finished. They are more likely to recall your speech if you conclude by summing up the main points (in the informative speech) or reiterating what you want them to do (in the persuasive speech).

Strange as it may seem, it is often useful to develop the body and conclusion of a speech first, saving the introduction for last. The body of the speech progresses logically to the conclusion, in a natural sequence. But you won't know what shape your introduction will take until you have the body and conclusion worked out; in other words, you can't write the introduction until you know what you are introducing.

In the process of arriving at his specific purpose, Tom has also worked out the content and organization of the body of his talk, as indicated in the previous pages. He will probably use the problem-solving approach and explain how to check certain parts of a used car while it is in the lot: rusting, body, tires, mileage, and upholstery. Let us turn now to the remaining portions of his talk—the introduction and conclusion—and examine the role they play in unifying his message. Though Tom would work on his conclusion first, for our purposes here it makes sense to begin with the introduction.

INTRODUCTION

If Tom were to begin by saying, "First we can look at the odometer to see how much the car has been driven," his listeners would be confused. They would have no way of knowing why he was suddenly discussing cars and odometers. They would feel, rightly, that he had left something out: the part of the speech that helps his audience tune in on the subject.

When you step up to give a speech, you need to remember that your listeners are a collection of individuals thinking their private thoughts about whatever seems most important to them at the moment. Your initial task is to provide them with a perspective on your topic that will closely parallel your own; then you can proceed to the meat of your message, and they'll be able to follow what you say. An easy way to provide that perspective is to explain how you became interested in your topic yourself. This beginning not only directs their thoughts toward your topic; it also directs their attention to you—the first of several goals your introduction should try to fulfill. A second goal, according to speech experts, is to acquaint your audience with the scope of your subject. Third, you want them to feel friendly toward you. You can attract attention by setting off a firecracker, but the involuntary reaction this produces would serve no useful purpose. You want the voluntary attention of your audience *throughout* the speech, and you must capture it at the outset by interesting them in you and your topic. How? By appealing to their needs and desires. This is where audience analysis comes in handy.

For a topic such as Tom's, no in-depth audience analysis is called for. He can assume that most people in his audience would desire an automobile for transportation to jobs, school, and social activities. He might also rightly deduce that most people have some hesitation when purchasing a used car because they want to find one that will be fairly economical to run and won't fall apart two weeks after they buy it. Given the strong wish most people have to own their own car, combined with their reluctance to get stung when purchasing one, Tom might appeal to both feelings in his opening sentences and accomplish the objectives of a good introduction at the same time. For example, he might use the popular technique of the rhetorical question (one for which you expect no answer from the audience): "I wonder how many of you are faced with a problem I've had—you're tired of waiting half an hour for a bus to get to school every day, you can't afford a new car, but you don't want to get a used one because you don't know much about mechanical things and you're afraid the salesman will gyp you. Well, I think I've come across a pretty foolproof way to take some of the guess-work out of buying a used car that I'd like to pass along to you today." Notice that, using this device, the speaker has attracted the audience's attention and taken the first step to focusing that attention on his topic (two of the objectives of the introduction); he also has taken the first step toward generating a friendly feeling toward himself. Putting it another way, he has begun to establish his credentials to speak on this topic by saying, in effect, "I think I have come across the solution to a problem we all share." The propagandist calls this the "plain folks" technique, meaning simply that the speaker establishes himself as no different from anybody else.

In the following pages we shall present other ways of introducing a speech topic that also accomplish the three goals outlined above. Some of these will be applicable to Tom's topic, others won't. Many can be used in combination with others. Many, as we point out later, can be used to handle the conclusion to a speech as well as the introduction. Study the examples carefully and see if you can adapt them to your topic. The discussion following each example should guide you in making a choice.

References to a recent incident. It may be that a recent incident, either something that happened to you personally or, better still, a news event your audience would know about too, can serve as a springboard into the topic of your talk. Perhaps such an incident inspired your choice of topic in the first place; then you need only describe the incident and point up its relation to your subject. In other cases, an incident that occurred after you had selected a topic and prepared the bulk of your speech may prove useful because of its relevance, timeliness, or appropriateness to the needs of your audience. For example, a confrontation between rebellious prisoners and city police could serve to focus your audience's attention on speeches designed to describe prison subcultures, prison conditions, police recruiting procedures, police training methods, police salaries, Black Power in prisons, or the like. Depending on the specific body of information you wished to present, you would pick an incident that best illustrated the problem or issue you wish to discuss. For Tom's purposes, an incident in which he or a friend had had difficulty or unusual success in selecting a used car would be ideal. Like most of the other techniques we will discuss here, this is a common opening in everyday conversation. Editorials in the daily press often begin this way also, as do many of our letters to friends and family.

References to the occasion, place, or previous speaker. This technique is most appropriate when the purpose of the speech is directly related either to the occasion for the gathering, such as a class reunion or a club meeting, or to the place where the gathering is held—the dedication of a new clubhouse, church, or stadium. Sometimes, speakers refer to the occasion, place, or previous speaker as an initial means of focusing the audience's attention on them or their subjects; or, they attempt to establish common ground with the audience or the previous speaker, who was able to establish rapport with the audience. Frequently, however, such references are included as part of the expected social amenities before you move on to your prepared introduction. Of course, if it is possible to blend the amenities with a smooth approach to your subject, so much the better. The clergyman who sought to outline the future growth and development of his newly dedicated church would be off to a good start if he referred to the pride his congregation had in their new building and the amount of self-sacrifice it took to realize their dream. He could easily build on those two feelings as he described his plans and his audience's involvement in them.

Rhetorical question. The rhetorical question—one you expect the audience to answer in their own minds, not aloud—is an excellent way to focus your listener's attention on the central idea of your speech. You can ask a single rhetorical question to achieve the effect, or a series of questions leading to the specific topic. For example, if your topic were "How to Handle Fire Emergencies in the Home," you could ask simply, "Do you know what you would do if you were awakened by a fire in your home tonight?" Or, to help your listeners zero in on the specific sub-points of your subject, you might employ a series of questions like these: "If you were awakened by fire tonight, which of the following things should you do first: (1) try to get out of the house as soon as possible? (2) try to locate the fire? (3) awaken others in the building? (4) call the fire department? (5) try to put the fire out?"

As you can see, the series not only serves to intensify attention by revealing the complexities of the problem; it can further serve to "outline" the speech for your audience in advance. This outlining function, also known as previewing, partitioning, and foreshadowing, makes your speech easier to follow. It is especially desirable in the informative speaking message, where you have no reason to withhold the goal of your speech from the audience. In some persuasive speeches—especially where the audience is hostile to you, your topic, or your purpose—you may find it advantageous to withhold your objectives until you are into the body or the conclusion of your speech. Writers of "how-to" articles for popular magazines like to begin with a series of rhetorical questions, because it helps them structure the body of the article while also making it easier for their readers to assimilate the information. Tom, as we noted, would find this a useful way to focus his audience's attention on the scope of his speech, at the same time explaining his own interest and background in the subject.

Startling statement. Startling statements, or "shockers" as they are sometimes called, are primarily useful in initial attempts to gain audience attention quickly and rivet it on a specific point. Tom, for example, might begin by saying "Many of you may think that buying a used car is like gambling—the house always wins. Well, I'm about to show you five ways you can beat the house at its own game."

When "shockers" are combined or contrasted with statements of a more pleasant or disarming nature, the power can be heightened. You will find them useful too in helping to establish a mood. Consider the effect the following statement might have: "As I look out over this sea of friendly, smiling faces [disarming pleasantry], I find it hard to believe that one in four of you will contract a form of cancer at some time in your lives. And if that weren't bad enough, the American Cancer Society's statistics indicate that if you do contract this dread disease, you have only two chances in six of surviving it."

Ordinarily, mood is most important in the persuasive speech, where the speaker wants to stimulate his audience to do something. As we said earlier, however, setting the right mood may help the informative speaker get his message across too. Tom, for example, could begin by citing some statistics on the frequency of repairs for cars over five years old that might jar his audience into a receptive mood for the information he had to share.

Quotations. The use of a quotation in his introduction can help the speaker accomplish several goals. Like other openings, it can serve initially to attract attention and help to focus that attention on specific ideas or aspects of the material you wish to present. In addition, however, this particular technique can help establish the importance or seriousness of your subject or purpose. The carefully chosen quotation—one attributed to a widely recognized figure who is known for his expertise in the matter you're discussing—can confirm or reinforce (1) the approach you have adopted for that discussion, (2) the need to talk about the subject, (3) the validity of the data you are presenting, and (4) the conclusions you draw from the data. Obviously, (3) and (4) would be more applicable to persuasive speeches, while (1) and (2) lend themselves more to informative speeches.

It should be pointed out also that certain quotations can startle or shock as well as suggest the importance of the problem or occasion. The techniques we are describing are interrelated and need not be used only in isolation.

Tom could easily find quotations that would serve his purpose in car or consumer magazines. Every spring articles appear in such magazines that outline methods for selecting a used car, any of which would contain quotable material.

Anecdotes. The anecdote, a narrative of an experience or incident that is relevant to the topic under discussion, can be serious or humorous. This technique is a natural for introductions because of the built-in appeal most stories hold for audiences. A well-chosen and well-told story can capture attention, hold it through the length of the story, and then focus it on a specific theme in the speech to follow.

Most textbooks caution novice speakers on the use of humor in their speeches, perhaps with good reason. Too many beginners, and some veterans who should know better, feel that any kind of joke, related to the topic or not, is all right since it puts the audience in a good mood. This logic is false on two counts. First, all parts of the speech should be related to the purpose, and an irrelevant joke obviously is not; secondly, many people simply cannot be funny when they are trying to be. There is little sense in risking the embarrassment of a joke that misfires at a time when you want to be on top of a situation. If you are a natural storyteller and life-of-the-party type, then by all means make use of your talents; but be sure your anecdote is relevant to your topic. Tom may be able to tell a great story about his last fishing trip, but his topic is purchasing a used car and the relationship between story and speech must not appear strained.

Illustration. The illustration, a term used interchangeably with anecdote, can be factual (like the anecdote) or hypothetical. The hypothetical illustration is useful because, rather than having to comb your memory or the newspapers to illustrate a point, you can create your own to fit your purposes and the interests of your audience. The speaker wishing to explain some rudiments of first aid could present us with this hypothetical illustration: "Suppose while walking to school this morning you came to a light-controlled intersection. You were tempted to sprint across and beat the changing light but some sixth sense warned you, and you stopped to wait for the next walk light. But the fellow who had been walking just ahead of you decided to gamble and almost made it across the street, except for the accelerating car that caught his coattail and flipped him into the side of a parked car. There he is lying awkwardly with his neck bent at a grotesque angle, cars streaming past, people gathering around clucking helplessly—he obviously needs help and fast—would you know what to do?" Notice that this hypothetical illustration is combined with the rhetorical question and the startling statement. Attention is caught, held, and focused on what you are about to say. All the technique requires is a little imagination and careful structuring to make it relevant to your purpose. If our faithful friend Tom put his imagination to work he could place us (figuratively speaking) on a used-car lot faced with a problem he could help us solve.

A WORD ABOUT TRANSITIONS

Before you can get from the introduction to the body of your speech—and from there to your conclusion—you'll need to give some thought to the fine art of linking each part smoothly to the next: the art of making a good transition. A transition is a verbal bridge that helps the reader or listener follow the sender from point to point and helps him to see the connections between those points. Careful attention to your classmates' speeches should reveal that quite often it is this ability to shift from point to point smoothly and logically that can make one speaker sound so much better than another, even though both have equally interesting topics and are otherwise equally prepared. Taking as an example the illustration mentioned above, the speaker might make his transition in this manner (transitions are italicized):

Suppose while walking to school this morning you came to a light-controlled intersection. You were tempted to sprint across and beat the changing light but some sixth sense warned you, and you stopped to wait for the next walk light. But the fellow who had been walking just ahead of you decided to gamble and almost made it across the street except for the accelerating car that caught his coattail and flipped him into the side of a parked car. There he is, lying awkwardly with his neck bent at a grotesque angle, cars streaming past, people gathering around clucking helplessly—he needs help and fast—would you know what to do?

Assuming you were not one of those fast-growing numbers of people who is afraid to "get involved," there are at least five things you can do even for a victim who is in as bad condition as this one seems to be.

One, send someone to call for an ambulance; two, get someone to direct traffic around him so he doesn't get hit again; three, keep the victim warm to counteract shock; four, clear his mouth of any obstructions so he can breathe; five, keep other well-intentioned amateurs from moving him and possibly injuring him further or killing him.

Now let's look at these commandments in greater detail.

As you can see, the transitions used here keep the thought flowing along, while also preparing the audience for the material to follow. This gives the listener a sense of continuity. Without the transitions, the speech would have a choppy sound and the audience would have to scramble trying to relate the various points you are presenting. Simply stated, the transitions help to make the audience's job easier, and isn't that what good communication is all about?

CONCLUSION

The conclusion of a speech determines whether or not it is successful just as much as the introduction or the body. It is the last thing the audience will hear you say on the subject—and often the only thing they will remember about it. Like the introduction, it has more than one task to accomplish; and, also like the introduction, it can accomplish those tasks in more than one way.

In general, the conclusion may attempt to (1) sum up the main and/or supporting points of the speech; (2) reinforce the credibility and favorable image of the speaker; and (3) in the persuasive speech, either instruct the audience on the specific course of action you want them to follow, or repeat the specific belief or attitude you want to instill, reinforce, or change. In short, the conclusion is directly linked to the specific purpose of the speech; it is not something extra, tacked on at the end, but rather the point to which the speech logically leads.

As we said earlier, many if not all of the techniques of beginning a speech can serve to conclude it as well. References to the occasion, to the previous speaker, to a recent incident can be used successfully at either end of the speech. So can quotations, questions, illustrations, and anecdotes. We don't mean to suggest that you are obligated to use the same technique as both the opening and closing device of the same speech—ordinarily, you would do well to consider using a variety of techniques. There are instances, however, where the same device serves in both spots. A reference in the conclusion to the same quote or illustration used to begin the speech is an effective way of tying the whole speech together.

As a general rule of thumb, the following are the more commonly accepted concluding techniques.

Summary. The informative speech in its simplest form involves: (1) telling your audience what you're going to tell them (introduction); (2) telling them about the subject (body); and (3) repeating your main points (conclusion). The conclusion in this instance is a simple summary of the body. You either repeat the main points in the same language you used in the speech or restate them in other language. This kind of conclusion is effective with the demonstration speech, or any straightfoward process description such as our first-aid speech or Tom's "purchasing a used car" speech.

Question. Regardless of the type of introduction employed, the question remains an effective closing device for a speech that has taken a historical approach to a topic. For example, a speech describing the increasing sophistication of transportation fuels might conclude in this way:

> We have seen that in the space of little more than a century, human technology has developed fuels to power our vehicles that range from the mundane to the exotic. From the days of the hayburner and steam engine we have progressed to the petroleum-based fuels, and in just the last twenty-five years to nuclear fission and derivatives of liquid oxygen and hydrogen. If the ionization process works, who knows what the fuel of the twenty-first century will be?

Charge to the audience. As mentioned above, in the persuasive speech you might conclude by charging the audience with a future responsibility; for example, the clergyman who admonishes his congregation to "Love thy neighbor as thyself!" or the coach who reminds his team "It's not whether you win or lose, but how you play the game that counts."

Request for immediate action. The persuasive speech that tries to make the audience do something usually closes with a request for immediate action, such as "Give till it hurts" or "March with me to city hall and we'll show 'em who's boss!"

Everyday Applications of Speech Techniques

As may be obvious by now, our friend Tom can conclude his speech in any number of ways. Not only that, there are innumerable ways to develop the body, introduction, and conclusion into a unified speech. The pattern of his speech, then, depends largely on the strength of his imagination and the control he exercises over it.

Equally important, as we pointed out earlier, all these techniques can be applied to an endless variety of informal, everyday communications in which we do not "give a speech." We can use the familiar organization patterns as easily in a sales conference as in an informative talk to a large group. The techniques for introductions and conclusions would be as valuable in individual conversations and conferences as they would in a talk before the local Rotary Club. At a party, Tom may run into a friend who is interested in buying a good secondhand car. He could start out with an anecdote about his own experiences with car buying, describe his checklist system as a solution to the problem, and conclude with a well-focused question. The basic principles of speech-making apply to the everyday situations because the task is still the same: to inform the receiver effectively.

Summary

There are significant differences between the informative and persuasive messages, whether they are spoken or written. Yet the speaker or writer can often successfully apply the principles of one to the other.

The informative spoken message is most successful when the speaker can do two things: (1) identify a specific purpose in relation to his audience, his knowledge of the subject, the time limits for the occasion, and the unique nature of the occasion itself; and (2) create a precise organization—in relation to the specific purpose and topic—for the body of the message and in the message as a whole. The effective speaker can use these techniques in everyday, informal situations as well as in more formalized speech situations.

Assignments

1. Make a list of five topics you are fairly familiar with, and

would enjoy speaking about. Select two or three organizational patterns you might employ for the body of an informative speech on each topic. Be able to defend your choices orally.

2. For each of the topics you have listed, prepare a statement of specific purpose that would be appropriate for a five-minute speech.

3. Select two or three of the topics on your list and do enough preliminary research to determine which of them you could speak about most effectively. Then prepare a five-minute speech on that topic.

4. Prepare a short oral report describing an effective speech you heard recently. Be able to explain why the content of the speech was well-adapted to the audience.

5. Bring to class the text of a speech that you think has an especially effective introduction. Keeping in mind the audience for whom the speech was intended and the topic of the speech, explain why this introduction is such a good one.

6. Look through various anthologies of famous speeches in your school's library, and find examples of each of the organizational patterns described in this chapter. Write a short explanation of how each pattern fits the topic the speaker was discussing.

7. Be prepared to assume the role of Tom in a classroom conversation that would simulate Tom's discussion with a friend about buying a used car. Apply the formal theory explained in this chapter to that informal conversation.

7

The Informative
Message
in Written
Communication

- THE DATA SHEET
- TWO BUSINESS LETTERS
- THE MEMO
- THE RESEARCH REPORT

HAVING ANALYZED the informative spoken message, let us apply some of the points considered in that discussion to writing situations. It will probably come as no surprise to you that most of these principles are equally relevant in both cases. Whether the occasion is formal or informal, whether you are writing for one person or for many, you will still need to identify a specific purpose and organize your ideas in a suitable form. Writers have to spend as much time preparing as do speakers, sorting through what they know about the subject, deciding what they can handle in the available space, and calculating the specific reactions of their readers.

For example, consider how you proceed to give someone written directions to your house. Let's say that person is a friend of yours from out of town who is coming to visit your new home for the first time and needs directions to get there easily. This informative task will take some care; you suddenly realize how hard it is for an outsider to grasp the familiar landmarks and street patterns of your city. You sit down and consider the various methods of organizing your directions so that your visitor can follow them without trouble. You might, for example, have him follow the route signs on the highways and then the street signs when he gets near your house. But you yourself have had enough bad experiences following signs in strange cities to realize that such directions are only partially adequate.

You reconsider. Your friend is an advertising salesman. Perhaps it would help if you identified some specific ads—billboards, big signs and the like, ones that will not change—along the route. These ads will help him verify that he is on the right routes and streets. Should you try to have him follow both the routes and the ads, though? Perhaps having him do both will be more confusing than helpful? In the end you decide to be very selective about the ads. You will use the route and street orientation, but you will also identify certain distinctive ads along the route at places where he will not have to worry about turning or heavy traffic.

As an additional aid, you decide to try to spot potential trouble spots along the way. There is a tricky turnoff at the junction of Route 18 and Aberg Avenue, for instance. And on

Aberg Avenue your friend will want to anticipate the left-turn lane, particularly if he happens to arrive during the rush-hour traffic. And where should your friend park? There is a spot for guests in the parking lot of your apartment building. Better tell him about that too.

Having sorted through all these ideas, you finally sit down to write the instructions. You put your three ideas in an order of importance. Your first paragraph gives street and route directions, your second paragraph spots the ads, your third details the trouble spots. When your friend receives the directions, he finds they are very understandable. When he comes to visit, he finds they are very workable. You have done your job of getting across the informative message.

The same principles you applied here will also serve in numerous other situations, like the five occupation-related informative messages discussed below.

The Data Sheet

Let's say that you are applying for a job, and the employing company has asked you to provide a data sheet, an organized summary of your job qualifications. The general purpose of such data sheets is to provide a prospective employer with a good deal of information about you in a short space. As a sender, you are supplying relevant data—hence the name *data sheet*.

But identifying a general purpose, as we have pointed out, is not good enough. You must identify a specific goal if you are to communicate well. That involves considering both the job you're applying for and your qualifications for it.

In this case assume that you are a man named Edward Van Buren. You are applying for a position as an art director with an advertising firm.

Before you sit down to write, you do some thinking. You consider the job first of all. "It's a director's job," you remind yourself, "and that calls for both educational training and a lot of experience. That company isn't going to hire anybody who's green or unskilled. Probably they're more interested in work experience than in an educational record, but both are important."

You then consider your own qualifications. You've had a good educational background, you think, and you're in good health. Your work record is solid. In school you even got some academic honors. Your hobbies indicate that you're fairly versatile—oh, and you were a staff artist of your college paper. You've got some good job references too, people who will vouch for your ability. You know how to type—you did clerical work in the navy. All of these thoughts go through your mind at random.

Sorting through these details, you decide on a specific purpose: to emphasize your work record and your schooling.

Your next task is to decide what to include to achieve that purpose, and here you put in the details relevant to the job. You worked as a camp counselor for two summers while you attended your community college, but that has almost nothing to do with an art director's position, so you leave it out. There's no point either in going back to high school since that was so long ago, except to indicate any job-related activities or academic honors. Your work on your high school and college papers as staff artist is definitely important, and so is your interest in photography, since the art director's job might involve doing photographic work. Also, you'll certainly want to mention that you were the outstanding commercial arts student at Whitney Junior College. And it is essential to describe your present job.

Now you organize. Using an old but tested rule of the business world, you put your work experience and educational background at the top of the data sheet, in separate categories (after the usual information about address, place of birth, etc.). In this way you "headline" your most significant qualifications. Below those two categories you include other relevant ones, arranging and grouping information in a logical way. Academic honors come after education, for example, and information regarding health and clerical skills is grouped under a miscellaneous category entitled Other Relevant Data. At the very end of the data sheet you put in another crucial category, your list of people who will vouch for your working abilities and responsibility. In this way you leave your reader, the receiver, with an appropriate ending, a further point about your employment background.

Your data sheet now looks like Figure 4. While it may not be the best data sheet ever written, its chances of success are good because you, the writer/sender, kept in mind the two principles for creating an effective, informative message.

Two Business Letters

But let's change the situation now. Suppose, for example, that you are a partner in a small insurance business. A man named Mr. Ward called you on Thursday of this week to take out additional car insurance with you. You thanked him, discussed the specific coverage, and told him that he was fully insured by your company from that time. Now, as the state law requires, you must write him a letter to confirm that conversation.

As a sender your specific purpose is not to "just write him a letter." Your specific purpose here is to inform Mr. Ward that his· additional coverage went into effect as soon as he notified you of his intent to purchase it. That is the main information of your message. As a secondary point, reinforcing the main one, you can inform Mr. Ward that he will be billed as of the day of the phone call, and the company will send him a notice to that effect.

You organize these two separate points in separate paragraphs. Since the point about the effective date of coverage is more important, that will be in the first paragraph. The point about billing is less crucial, so that will follow the first one.

You also put in a third paragraph, a "courtesy statement" thanking Mr. Ward, your receiver, and offering your services in the future. This is necessary, but since it is the least important item, it will go last in the overall organization. When finished, your letter looks like Figure 5.

For another illustration, let's assume that you are employed as the manager of a store that sells stereophonic equipment for

PERSONAL DATA SHEET

Edward Van Buren   Born: 1/7/43
1019 W. Main St.   Military status: inactive
Waco, Texas 83714   reserve
Phone 222-2626   Marital status: married

Work Experience

    1963-1965 Salesman, Sony Corp. (Houston,
      Texas)
    June, 1967- Advertising artist, Neil's
      Merchandise World (Waco, Texas)

Education

    Associate Degree in Commercial Arts, Whitney
      Junior College (Whitney, Okla.),
      June, 1967
    Diploma, Jerrot High School (Jerrot, Okla.),
      June, 1961

Honors

    Outstanding Commercial Arts Student, Whitney
      Jr. College, 1967
    Member, National Honor Society, Jerrot High
      School

Extracurricular Activities

    Whitney Jr. College: artist and advertising
      manager, The Reporter
      member, Student Senate
      co-chairman, Awards Day Program, 1967
    Jerrot H. S.: staff artist, The Maroon

Figure 4. Personal Data Sheet

Other Relevant Details

Excellent health
Knowledge of typing and office skills as a result of clerical assignment in U. S. Navy
Hobbies: photography and electronics

References

Mr. J. H. Green, Advertising Manager, Neil's Merchandise World, P. O. Box 531, Waco, Texas
Mr. Arthur Statz, Sales Manager, Sony Corp., 112 Westchester Dr., Houston, Texas
Mr. Ralph Bronson, Instructor in Commercial Arts, Whitney Jr. College, Whitney, Okla.

Figure 4. Personal Data Sheet (*cont.*)

the home. Some months before, you contracted with a major manufacturer for the franchise to sell its goods exclusively in your city.

Since the time you signed the contract some problems have come up regarding its interpretation. One of these involves the matter of discounts to customers. The contract provides that your store cannot discount more than 20% below prices set by the company. But three kinds of headphone the company supplies have not been listed on the price sheet accompanying the contract. "Is this an oversight," you wonder, "or are the headphones discountable beyond 20%?"

Another problem concerns damaged merchandise. Your contract with the company specifies that the company will repair all such merchandise and will reimburse you for all your shipping costs. However, in some cases the cost of the shipping has been very high. You wonder if it would not have been wiser to

INDIANA CAR AND ACCIDENT COMPANY

ICA

715 N. Randolph Place / Muncie, Indiana 45721

June 5, 1974

Mr. R. P. Ward
19 S. Baldwin Ave.
Muncie, Indiana

Dear Mr. Ward,

This is to confirm our telephone conversation of
last Thursday, during which I told you that your
additional insurance became effective as of that
date. You have been fully insured since Thursday,
according to the terms we discussed.

We have sent to National Casualty Company a form
detailing the additional coverage you requested.
You should be receiving in a week or two their
premium notice and bill for the additional amount.
You will be billed as of last Thursday.

As always it is a pleasure to do business with
you. If I can be of any service at any time, call
me or come into the office.

Sincerely,

Janet E. Barnes

Janet E. Barnes

JEB:lt

Figure 5. Sample Confirmation Letter

have the merchandise fixed locally, thus saving the manufacturer shipping costs and your firm time in returning the goods to the customer. The contract mentions nothing about such a course of action, but you would like to know the company's feeling about this matter. Specifically, you would like to know if the manufacturer would reimburse you for reliable repair work done locally.

Another problem concerns advertising. Under the terms of your agreement, the company was to furnish free of charge to you all fliers, brochures, and specification sheets for their products. You have received these items in the mail, but you have also received 200 copies of a longer, fifty-page booklet entitled *Buying Stereophonic Equipment: Baton Answers Your Questions.* For these booklets you were billed, even though you considered them in the same category as the other materials. "Is this a billing error?" you ask yourself. "Why shouldn't the booklets be considered advertising like the other items? They're distributed to the buying public for nothing too."

Still another matter concerns prices on merchandise being phased out by the company. The contract specifies that you can charge lower than normal prices on these goods, but a question arises about this situation: When is a merchandise item old? As soon as the company notifies you by mail that a new product is available? Or when the new products arrive in your store? The difference between these two definitions could mean a great deal in terms of your store's profits.

Rethinking all of this, you decide on a specific purpose for your letter. You conclude that all the items relate to your agreement with the company, and that there are four problems:

1. headphone price discounts;
2. damaged goods;
3. billing for advertising booklets;
4. pricing of phased-out merchandise.

Therefore your specific purpose is to discuss four problems of the contract. That will be stated in your opening paragraph.

Then you decide how to organize the rest of the letter. Reviewing for a moment again, you notice that all the matters are involved enough to be treated individually, in separate paragraphs. You notice also that the first and fourth matters are related to each other; they both involve price discounts. So you can put these points next to one another.

Should these paired paragraphs be first in the letter? or last? or sandwiched between the remaining two points in their separate paragraphs? You consider a moment and then decide: "Well, all of the matters are of equal importance. As far as overall organization goes, all I can really do to get the message across better to the receiver is to put in that opening summary paragraph and then group the two pricing paragraphs together. Oh, and I'd better leave a last paragraph thanking the company in advance for answering my letter—courtesy always helps." Your letter, then, with its identifiable specific purpose and suitable organization, looks like Figure 6.

The Memo

We change the situation again. In this case your name is Chester Ramsey, and you are employed as an office manager in a firm that manufactures fire-fighting equipment.

The time is early July. In May of this year you had a meeting with all your department heads, and one of the items discussed at that time was business institutes. You mentioned at the meeting that attending such institutes was a good way of keeping up on developments in various fields, and you urged all department heads to submit lists of appropriate institutes employees might attend. "Submit your request to Mr. Rusk," you said at the time, "so that he can budget accordingly."

One week ago Mr. Rusk sent a note to you saying that he had received lists from only half of the departments. Despite the fact that he had reminded the department heads in a memo, requests were not coming in.

You decide to take action. You will write a memo yourself.

In this case the specific purpose of the message is fairly easy to identify: you will urge the department heads to get the requests in as they were asked to do. But you redefine the purpose

SOUND WORLD INCORPORATED

11 Kedzie Road / Chicago, Illinois 47531

Dec. 17, 1974

Baton Sound Corporation
77 S. Sunset Avenue
New Plain, Pennsylvania 32045

Attn. Mr. Feldman

Dear Mr. Feldman:

Since Baton and I signed our franchise agreement, four matters have come
up involving its interpretation. I'd like you to clarify the company's
position on them.

The first matter concerns discounts on three kinds of headphones, the XS,
XX, and WY models. None of these is listed on the price sheet accompanying
the franchise agreement, and I wonder if this is an oversight or if these
headphones are excluded from the discount clause agreement. Could you give
me an answer to that question?

A second matter also concerns price discounts. Nothing in the franchise
contract defines when a product is old. Can I discount merchandise below
the 20% level when I receive notification by mail from you that the new
models are out? Or must I wait until I actually receive the new merchandise
in my store? The difference between those two definitions means a great
deal in the way I choose to market goods, as you can appreciate, I'm sure.

A third matter concerns damaged goods. I've been shipping marred or faulty
merchandise back to you, as the contract says I should do. However, on some
cases, I've noticed shipping costs have been very high. I wonder if it wouldn't
be cheaper for you and more convenient for me to have the damaged goods fixed
locally by a reliable repairman. This would save shipping costs for you, and
I could get the repaired merchandise back to my customers faster. I know there
is nothing in the contract about such an arrangement, but I would be willing to
try it for a while, for minor repairs, if you're in agreement.

Finally, I have a question about your booklets Buying Stereophonic Equipment:
Baton Answers Your Questions. I ordered 200 copies of these and received them.
But I was later billed for them. Correct me if I am wrong, but aren't these
booklets free advertising materials, covered by clause 13 of the contract?
Aren't they in the same category as fliers, brochures, and specifications sheets?

Thanks in advance for looking into these questions. I look forward to your
prompt reply.

Sincerely,

Ryan March

Ryan March, owner
RM/nt

Figure 6.   Sample Letter of Inquiry

slightly by setting a specific, final deadline—Friday of this week.

Having done that, you organize. You could use the standard business technique, you think, of putting the most important information in the first paragraph and the least important following that. But that wouldn't get across to the department heads the amount of time that has passed since the original directive was made to them. Neither would it emphasize how many times they had been reminded.

You decide on a different approach. You will summarize date by date (paragraph by paragraph) those occasions when the department heads were notified about institute requests. Going from the least recent to the most recent occasions, you will review for them their lack of attention to this matter.

Your organization pattern, then, is chronological order through most of the memo, leading up to the specific-purpose paragraph setting the new deadline, Friday. You will deliberately keep the main point near the end to build suspense—therefore interest. You also decide to include a final paragraph restressing why you think the institutes are so valuable. A minor point in this paragraph, to tone down the rest of the letter's bluntness, points out that the department heads may have had legitimate reasons, to a degree, in letting this oversight occur. When completed, your memo looks like Figure 7.

In all these business applications of the informative message, you notice, the specific purpose is readily identifiable. The artist applied for the art director's job by stressing his work record and schooling. The insurance agent wrote to inform Mr. Ward that his new coverage had gone into effect on a particular date. The store manager took up four matters involving the franchise contract. The office manager urged the department heads to get their requests in by a certain date.

In each case too, the organization depends on the purpose of the message. The data sheet writer put his most important material first, as Mr. Barnes did in writing to Mr. Ward—the method of organization is "most important to least important." The store manager's letter started with a purpose paragraph and then took up the four topics mentioned there—its overall organization is topical arrangement. In the memo the organization

To: All department heads   Date: July 6

From: C. Ramsey

Subject: Business institute lists

In a management meeting on May 3 you were asked
to compile a list of business institutes in
your special fields that your staff members could
attend. You may recall that you were also to
include with the lists a brief description of each
institute, giving dates, costs, and program
summaries.

In a memo dated May 17 you were asked to have
these lists forwarded to Mr. Rusk by June 1.

Some of you were reminded by Mr. Rusk on June 15,
according to a copy of his memo that I have,
that you had not turned these in.

I have a note on my desk from Mr. Rusk about a
variety of matters. It is dated June 28. In that
note Mr. Rusk informs me that he has received
lists from only half of the departments.

Would those of you who have not finished com-
piling these lists do so by Friday at the latest?
Mr. Rusk is trying to budget these items, but
he cannot do this realistically until all of the
lists have come in.

I know this has been a busy time in our operations. We have all been working hard to get
our new FIREPAC rescue equipment on the market.
However, I don't think we can afford to overlook
the long-range benefits of business institutes.

Figure 7.   Sample Memo

```
Please see that Mr. Rusk gets the information
he needs.


JR:eb
cc: Mr. Rusk
```

Figure 7. Sample Memo (*cont.*)

was chronological, a time review showing how the department heads had consistently delayed getting their requests in.

Purpose and organization! Perhaps we are belaboring those points unnecessarily by now, but they are so crucial to good informative messages that they are worth reemphasizing. The more informative messages you speak or write, the more you will realize this. The more you can identify the very concrete purpose in your mind and the more you can arrange the material in a suitable pattern, then the more successful your message will be.

The Research Report

Let's take one last example as final proof of this. In this situation you are employed as an investigating specialist in a fairly large police department. You do laboratory and field work, gathering and interpreting scientific evidence.

Inspector Norton, the head of your division, has recently heard of a police technique using something called voiceprints, a method of permanently copying someone's voice on electronic equipment. He wonders if this voiceprinting technique, like fingerprinting, wouldn't be valuable in solving and prosecuting criminal cases. "Look into the possibility of using voiceprints as an investigative technique," he says. "Write a report making appropriate recommendations "

Your first step after getting these directions is to go to the library, where you will find relevant materials on the subject of voiceprinting. You've been to the library before, so you know the basic sources of information; you have in the back of your mind a quick summary of possible reference works to consult:

1. Encyclopedias—the subject of voiceprinting is so new that it probably will not be included here, but you'll look anyway.

2. The card catalog—this file cabinet indexing books by author, subject, and title may have important data, but like the encyclopedia it may not have much since the subject is a recent development; you'll check though.

3. *The Reader's Guide to Periodical Literature*—you've used this before so you know that it indexes magazine articles by author, subject, and title; you know, too, that the magazines tend to be general or popular while voiceprinting is pretty specialized; you may find here one or two articles on the subject but not too many.

4. *The Business Periodicals Index*—this is like *The Reader's Guide,* but it is more specialized. However, for you the specialization is too much in the area of business; you'll look here but won't expect to find much.

5. *The Applied Science and Technology Index*—this is like *The Reader's Guide* and *The Business Periodicals Index,* but you know that it specializes in indexing magazine articles about science and technology; this is probably going to be your best source of information.

6. Various indexes for magazines in more specialized fields; indexes for newspapers; pamphlet files listing documents, papers, and brochures published by the government and others—you'll check out each of these sources too; you may find something valuable in any one of them.

You get to work going through these materials. Before you do, though, you remind yourself about some special points affecting communication in a report like this, involving research. One of these is that the receiver of your report may want to verify for himself what you have written. Or, if he does not want to verify the information, he may want to just read more on the subject. At the least he wants to know what ideas or wording in the report are yours as opposed to someone else's.

In order to help him in this case, you as a sender can do a couple of things during your research. One is to develop a bibliography, a list of all the materials you used in arriving at your conclusions, alphabetized by the names of the authors of the materials. The simplest way to develop this is by listing each source on a note card, alphabetizing the cards later, and then typing the names on a single sheet of paper to go at the end of the report. With this list in hand your receiver can go himself to the library, either to verify your work or delve into the subject more on his own.

Second, you can make sure that every specialized idea you borrow from a source is credited to the person who came up with the idea. You do this by preparing footnote cards, identifying for each borrowed point the author, title of the book or article, date of publication, and the number of the page on which the idea was presented. These cards must be as accurate and complete as possible, to ensure that your footnotes will serve the purposes for which they are intended: (a) to tell the reader that material has been borrowed, and acknowledge the source of the information; (b) to give a specific page reference for borrowed material (as bibliographies do not), thus enabling the reader to locate the context of a quotation if he is interested; (c) to protect yourself from charges of plagiarism (using the ideas or words of another as your own).

Third, you can make sure that any specific phrases and statements you borrow word for word will be copied down and put in quotation marks on your footnote cards. You do this to make sure that any outstandingly phrased or well-summarized statement will be attributed later to the person who made it, not to you.

With these points in the back of your mind, you look for appropriate materials to take notes from. A couple of good sources appear in newspaper articles. You get a few more from some general magazines, and you dig up some good information from specialized periodicals. You also find an excellent scientific paper by the inventor of the voiceprint technique himself!

From these sources you collect ideas which you record on footnote cards, and out of these ideas you are able to redefine your specific purpose better. Your report will be directed toward one single thought: your department ought to look further into the use of voiceprinting since it may soon become an accepted technique of investigation and possibly prosecution. That is the main point to get across to Inspector Norton, your receiver. That is the logical conclusion of your research.

An organization pattern also emerges from your reading. You realize that you will have to explain first of all how voiceprinting works, since other ideas will all relate to the general theory of how a voice gets printed on a machine. Without this general knowledge, your receiver will not understand more specific points.

You realize also that that explanation can be made much clearer if you go into the history of voiceprinting, tracing the story from initial developments to the more sophisticated techniques in use today. The idea of using voiceprints, you learn, originated as early as World War II. Only in recent times, however, has it become an accepted identification technique.

Thinking about your reading, you also come up with two other organizational categories. One of these will describe the possible uses of voiceprinting, in annoying or obscene phone call cases, bomb scares, extortion, false fire alarms, and so on. The other will deal with the legality of voiceprinting in court, not just in terms of its admissibility as evidence but also in terms of its acceptance as reliable proof.

With most of your research done, you make up an organizational outline, which looks like this:

Voiceprinting

   I. Theory
   II. History
   III. Uses in criminal investigation
   IV. Legality
   V. Recommendations for our department

It's a topical outline, you realize. The overall subject is divided into various subheadings that pertain to it individually. These lead into the final recommendations.

Now you write your report. Keeping in mind your unifying idea, you direct your supporting paragraphs toward that goal. You make obvious your shifts in thought, and guide your reader along with transitions. You insert ideas you borrowed from your reading, and you include those word-for-word phrases and statements you copied, that expressed certain ideas better than you ever could have.

A couple of special questions come into your head when you insert these borrowed items. One concerns exactly how to indicate to your reader that some idea or wording is borrowed from a reading source.

The solution to that problem is to take your borrowed idea or wording from your footnote cards, insert it into your paper in the appropriate place, and then immediately following it put in a footnote number, a regular arabic number raised slightly above the line. This footnote number will be repeated at the end of your paper on a separate sheet of paper, and there it will be followed by the information saying where the idea or wording came from. This information could have been included right in the report, where you put the footnote number, but that would have made it hard for your receiver, the reader, to keep the continuity. So the footnote number is inserted and then explained later, at the end of the report, before the bibliography.

Let's see how this works in the report we've been talking about. For example, you borrowed an idea and some wording early in the report. You need to indicate this to your reader without destroying his train of thought, so you put in a footnote.

Borrowed Idea Inserted into Report

```
     Voiceprints are pictures of a person's

unique way of saying individual words. When a
```

persons speaks, voice energy is transmitted through the unique vocal cavities formed by the unique size and shape of his throat, nose, and mouth. It is therefore possible to identify the speaker of an individual word by the energy pattern he alone produces.[1]

Borrowed Wording

According to a statement in Bell Laboratories Record, voiceprints "reveal the unique patterns of voice energy in the various levels of pitch-- fundamental patterns that are quite distinctive and identifiable."[2]

At the end of the report, these footnote numbers are decoded as follows, telling your reader where the specific source of the borrowed idea or wording is:

1. "Voiceprints, Like Fingerprints, May be Unique and Almost Unchangeable," Sound 2 (January 1963): 54.

2. "Voice Spectograms are Unique Personal Identification," Bell Laboratories Record 40 (June 1962): 214.

A second question about inserting borrowed material concerns the insertion of quotes. Some of them can be worked right into your own sentences, since the borrowed phrases or words are short—you did this in the case of the second footnote item. But other quotes are longer. To thrust them into your own sentences would mean that your receiver, the reader, would never be able to figure out the main idea of a passage because he would lose the continuity.

The solution in this case is to "block" long quotations, that is, to indent the borrowed wording and single space it. When material is blocked this way, you need not put in quotation marks since the blocking indicates borrowed wording to your reader. Here is an example.

> The problems associated with Kersta's domination of the field have come to a head. Courts in the future may be reluctant to admit his testimony as a qualified expert. Extensive tests with controlled positive results will be necessary to overcome negative opinion in the scientific community. Finally, the prosecution in the future must be prepared to deal more effectively with theoretical problems underlying voiceprint technology . . . medical experts must testify as to physiological and anatomical matters. . . . The problems associated with voiceprints are fundamentally interdisciplinary in nature and will require for their solution the efforts of medical men, linguists, lawyers, and engineers.[16]

A problem related to maintaining continuity while quoting concerns dropping and adding material to a quote. In the first case there may be material in the quote that is unnecessary to your particular purpose. In that instance you need not include it. But how do you indicate to your reader that you've tampered with the quote?

The answer is to use the ellipsis, three spaced periods that indicate an omission. You don't need to place ellipsis dots at the beginning of a quotation, because the reader will assume that something came before the particular extract that you are using in your report. You need them at the end only if you are leaving out part of the last sentence. But if you are omitting a few words or an entire sentence or more from the middle of a quotation, you need to indicate this with the three dots, as shown in the blocked quote above. In the first case, he has deleted only part of a sentence, so three dots are all he needs to use. In the second case, the deleted material was a sentence or more, so the report writer has added a fourth period to indicate the end of the sentence preceding the omission.

Sometimes it is necessary to *add* a few words to a quote: to clarify it, to make it fit in smoothly with your own words, or to correct an error in the wording. The way to indicate these additions is to enclose them in brackets [ ], as in the following example:

```
"Voiceprints," one authority pointed out as

early as 1947, "could revolutionize [criminal]

detection."21
```

You observe all these specialized practices for communicating with your reader in a research report. However, the success of your report as an informative message is only partly due to your awareness of these rules. The major considerations for the writer of a good research paper are those of the other writers described in this chapter—to identify a specific purpose and develop a suitable organization. That's how you, as a sender, can get across a message about voiceprinting to your receiver. Following the summary and assignments for this chapter, we have included the finished report on voiceprint usage, to fully illustrate the principles explained above.

Summary

Like the effectively spoken informative message, the effectively written informative message both identifies the *specific purpose* of the message and finds a suitable *organization* for it. Both of these principles may be applied to a variety of occupational and nonoccupational situations.

Assignments

1. Unscramble all of the following information, and write a letter of request to the Johnson Co. Show that you understand the principles of identifying the specific purpose and organizing the ideas in a suitable form.

You are an executive with a firm named Yard-Goods, Inc. It is the fall of the year, and you need to know what winter materials your supplier, the E. E. Johnson Co., is going to have available for purchase. The Johnson Co. is located at 4438 E. 19th St. in Minneapolis, Minnesota. Your firm is located at 215 S. State Ave. in Pharo, N.Y. You are mainly interested in selling plaids and stripes, since they sold well in your area last year. The date on which you are thinking about all this is September 19. What you really need from the Johnson Co. is a copy of their seasonal catalog. You also feel that you should tell the Johnson Co. that their Dacrons have sold well. In fact, last year your sale of their Dacrons increased by 30%.

2. Applying the same principles that you used in assignment 1, write a memo. The situation is as follows: You work for the telephone company as a safety supervisor. In the last year in your company, accidents were most often attributed to faulty equipment, unsafe working conditions, and human carelessness. Of these three causes the one that showed up most frequently was the last. The date is March 19. In the last three months the rate of accidents has increased by 20%. You will be observing conditions and operations in the plant more closely in the next month. Your immediate concern, however, is to remind Mr. Portnoy, Ms. Bons, and Mr. Crabtree that they should alert

their employees to safety hazards. Their respective departments are Engineering, Development, and Manufacturing. Your boss is Mr. Ryan. The second most frequent cause of accidents was unsafe working conditions.

3. Write a data sheet in response to an ad for a specific job in your field. Clip the ad from a newspaper or trade journal, and attach it to your data sheet when you turn it in to your instructor. Once again, apply the principles of purpose and organization. (Keep a copy of your data sheet for the time when you actually do go job-hunting. It will probably serve as a very good foundation for the sheet you make up at that time.)

4. Write a report to the administration of your school on one of these problems: congested traffic in certain hallways, slow movement of elevators, inadequate or poor food in your cafeteria. If none of these problems occurs in your school, then find a problem to write about. Be thorough. Take surveys if you need to. You might interview people for their reactions. Identify specific trouble spots, and suggest specific remedies. Try to keep the report under three typewritten pages.

5. Present to your instructor a list of four potential topics for a technical research report related to your field. In cooperation with your instructor, narrow the list to one. Then go to the library, do research, and write the report, including footnotes and a bibliography. Make sure the research is complete. See to it that the report is directed toward a specific purpose by means of suitable organization.

6. Write a set of directions for assembling some fairly simple item around your house or apartment: a fishing reel, a transistor radio, a sewing buttonholer, a hair-dryer, a lamp, etc. Before you write the instructions, disassemble the object. Then write the instructions, but do not reassemble the object. Take the pieces to class and test your instructions on someone unfamiliar with the object. (A word of caution: make sure you understand the workings of whatever object you choose.)

Voiceprint Usage

To: Inspector Norton   Date: April 22, 1974

From: Captain Knowles

Subject: Voiceprints as a possible investigative

         technique

As you requested earlier this month, I've

recently done research into the possibility of

using voiceprinting in our investigative opera-

tions. Here is a summary of the findings.

The Theory of Voiceprinting

Voiceprints are pictures of a person's unique

way of saying individual words. When a person

speaks, voice energy is transmitted through his

unique vocal cavities, formed by the unique size

and shape of his throat, nose, and mouth. It is

therefore possible to identify the speaker of

an individual word by the energy pattern he alone

produces.[1] According to a statement in Bell Laboratories Record, voiceprints "reveal the unique patterns of voice energy in the various levels of pitch--fundamental patterns that are quite distinctive and identifiable."[2]

The leader in the voiceprinting field is L. G. Kersta, who developed a machine called a spectograph, which records the various energy patterns on paper in a kind of contour map of a word. Kersta claims that this voiceprint may be as valuable in criminal investigation as the fingerprint is. He envisions the day when criminals will be voiceprinted by saying the ten most commonly used English words: it, me, you, the, on, I, is, and, a, and too. These prints would be kept nationally at a central location where they could be stored by computer. Experts could then match unidentified prints from crime cases with those on file.[3]

History

Voiceprinting was actually conceived as early
as World War II, when scientists at Bell Labs
experimented with the idea of monitoring enemy
troop movement by taping radio voices and identifying them. Intelligence personnel thought that
by matching voiceprints at two different times
they could thus track enemy units. Not enough was
known about voice production at the time, however,
to make the idea workable, and it was not until
1960 that Bell Labs was able to develop the
contour voiceprint.[4] By 1962 Kersta, at Bell, had
made tests in which 25,000 voiceprints spoken by
25 people were analyzed by girl high school students who had been trained in five days. Kersta
reported that the girls were 97% accurate in
identifying the correct speaker.[5]

In recent years voiceprinting has been per-
fected to the point where Kersta now feels that a

trained expert can guarantee 99% accuracy.[6]
More significantly, the voiceprinting has been
widely adopted as an investigative method. To
quote a paper by Kersta distributed by his Voiceprint Laboratories:

> In law enforcement applications voice
> print identification assistance has been pro-
> vided for over 45 law enforcement agencies,
> including municipal, county, state, and
> government agencies. More than 250 individual
> cases have been processed for these agencies,
> and no report of error has occurred. Expert
> testimony has been given at six trials with
> favorable rulings of admissibility occurring
> in all . . .[7]

It would appear that voiceprinting is becoming an
accepted investigative technique.

Uses

Voiceprints have been used for a variety of
criminal cases: perjury, annoying phone calls,
obscene phone calls, bomb scares, arson, nar-
cotics, extortion, and false fire alarms.[8]

Another case, one of the first where voiceprinting
was used, was an investigation into an air crash
in 1964. Tapes from the plane's radio transmission
were sent to Voiceprint Laboratories where they
were made intelligible and analyzed. Investigation proved that the pilot and co-pilot had
been shot by an unidentified person.[9]

Perhaps the most devastating use of voiceprinting, however, came in 1966 following the
Watts riots. The accused person had appeared on
the CBS Reports program with his back to the
camera. In the interview he openly admitted
throwing a Molotov cocktail which destroyed a
drugstore. Partly on the basis of a voiceprint
analysis of the TV audio recording, the accused
was convicted.[10]

Legality

The main problem with voiceprinting to date--
despite Kersta's assertions about the admissibility of expert testimony on voiceprints--

has been its legality. According to William R. Jones in a recent <u>American Criminal Law Review</u> article, voiceprint identifications are not being admitted as evidence in most courts, even though voice identifications from nonexpert witnesses are commonly accepted. One reason Jones cites is the judges' fear that, because voiceprints are obtained by mechanical means, juries will assume they must be infallible. A nonexpert witness who identifies someone from the sound of his voice can be readily cross-examined, and flaws in his testimony pointed out to the jury. But when an expert witness is interpreting a sound specto-gram, presenting it as an accurate graphic recording of a person's voice, "the jury's ability to . . . evaluate its credibility may be seriously diminished."[11]

Of course, this fear would not exist if the courts were convinced that voiceprints were fully reliable. But appellate courts, as reported

by Ross E. Steinhauer in the Saturday Review,
have been inclined to agree with the scientists
who oppose Kersta on the grounds that his initial
sample tests were too limited.[12] William Jones
describes this opposition in greater detail:

> Experts in the fields of acoustics, linguis-
> tics, and phonetics have criticized both
> the design of [Kersta's] experiments and the
> scientific principles on which the technique
> relies, and they have generally refused to
> accept his claims of reliability.[13]

Another scientist, Dr. Oscar Tosi, tested Kersta's
assertions in a two-year study (completed in
1970) which "avoided most of the design faults
criticized in Kersta's experiments."[14] But even
though Tosi's study confirmed Kersta's findings,
it has had little effect as yet.

Two other reasons are given by Steinhauser for
the courts' unwillingness to accept Kersta's technique as a valid one. Kersta's lack of knowledge
about anatomy and physiology impairs his credibility; he is looked upon as an engineer rather

than engineer-physiologist. And Kersta has dominated the voiceprinting field to the point where he is suspected by defense lawyers of bias. As president of a private company which profits from voiceprint analysis, he has less acceptability than, say, an FBI fingerprint analyst with nothing to gain personally.[15]

Steinhauer summarizes the legal problems as follows:

> The problems associated with Kersta's domination of the field have come to a head. Courts in the future may be reluctant to admit his testimony as a qualified expert. Extensive tests with controlled positive results will be necessary to overcome negative opinion in the scientific community. Finally, the prosecution in the future must be prepared to deal more effectively with theoretical problems underlying voiceprint technology. . . . Medical experts must testify as to physiological and anatomical matters. . . . The problems associated with voiceprints are fundamentally interdisciplinary in nature and will require for their solution the efforts of medical men, linguists, lawyers and engineers.[16]

In all fairness, however, one ought to conclude
that eventually legality will cause few problems.
When prosecutors have more expert witnesses and
more diversified ones, when the results from more
extensive reliability samples become available,
test cases will undoubtedly be more favorable
to the voiceprinting technique.

Recommendations

This research into voiceprinting seems to
indicate two conclusions, noted below.

1. Voiceprinting seems to be advanced enough so
   that we would profit from sending one or more
   persons from our staff to the in-residence
   service program run by Voiceprint Laboratories.[17] While we may not be able to use
   voiceprint evidence extensively in court, we
   can use it a great deal in investigation. It
   would be instrumental in gaining confessions.
   Furthermore, if we were to publicize its use,

that publicity might serve as a deterrent
to some crimes, especially annoying or obscene
phone calls.

2. It would appear that there is a need for the
FBI to create a voiceprinting facility staffed
with experts, or to initiate plans for one
immediately. I suggest we query the FBI about
this.

REFERENCES

1. "Voiceprints, Like Fingerprints, May Be Unique and Almost Unchangeable," Sound 2 (January 1963): 54.

2. "Voice Spectograms Are Unique Personal Identification," Bell Laboratories Record 40 (June 1962): 214.

3. "Voiceprints, Like Fingerprints," 54.

4. "Voice Spectograms," 214-15.

5. "Voices Don't Lie," Newsweek 59 (June 4, 1962): 62.

6. L. G. Kersta, "Voiceprint Identifications in Law Enforcement," paper distributed by Voiceprint Laboratories, 2.

7. Ibid., 2.

8. Ibid., 2.

9. "Death Call of Airliner's Co-Pilot," San Francisco Chronicle (June 4, 1964): 24.

10. "TV Remarks Lead to Watts Riot Conviction," Los Angeles Times (December 10, 1966): 3.

11. William R. Jones, "Danger--Voiceprints Ahead," The American Criminal Law Review 11 (Spring 1973): 554.

12. Ross E. Steinhauer, "Voice Prints: A New Aid in Detecting Criminals," Saturday Review 52 (September 6, 1969): 56-59.

13. Jones, 551.

14. Ibid., 553.

15. Steinhauer, 56-59.

16. Steinhauer, 59.

17. Kersta, 5.

BIBLIOGRAPHY

"Death Call of Airliner's Co-Pilot." San Francisco
Chronicle (June 4, 1964): 24.

Jones, William R. "Danger--Voiceprints Ahead."
The American Criminal Law Review 11 (Spring
1973): 549-73.

Kersta, L. G. "Voiceprint Identification in Law
Enforcement." Paper distributed by Voiceprint
Laboratories, Farrington Manufacturing Co.,
Somerville, New Jersey.

Steinhauer, Ross E. "Voice Prints: A New Aid in
Detecting Criminals." Saturday Review 52
September 6, 1969): 56-59.

"TV Remarks Lead to Watts Riot Conviction."
Los Angeles Times (December 10, 1966): 3.

"Voiceprints, Like Fingerprints, May Be Unique
and Almost Unchangeable." Sound 2 (January
1963): 54-55.

"Voices Don't Lie." Newsweek 59 (June 4, 1962):
62.

"Voice Spectograms Are Unique Personal Identification." Bell Laboratories Record 40 (June
1962): 214-15.

8

The Persuasive Message in Spoken Communication

As YOU MAY HAVE noted while studying the examples we provided in the last two chapters, the *purely* informative message is a rare one. Certainly, most of our daily spoken communication is primarily persuasive, and it is the nature of these communications that we shall discuss here. Consider your most recent conversation. You or those you were talking with were probably trying to convince somebody about something. As a persuader you had one or more goals: trying to *instill* an attitude, trying to *reinforce* an attitude that already existed, or trying to *change* an existing attitude. After manipulating your listener's attitude in any of these ways you might have wanted him to demonstrate his acceptance, reinforcement, or change in attitude by doing something. You were like the salesman who tried to convince you his product was best, so you would buy it.

Most authorities believe that such manipulation of attitude (persuasion) is accomplished through a combination of three persuasive elements: personal impression (image), reason, and appeals to the emotions.

For our purposes in this chapter, then, *persuasion* may be defined as *the deliberate attempt to instill, reinforce or change attitudes or behavior by means of personal impression (image), reason, and appeals to the emotions.* Our discussion will focus on: (1) how attitudes are formed and protected; (2) the various goals of persuaders; and (3) the three elements that may be employed in any persuasive act. The chapter will conclude with some suggested persuasive strategies and a sample dialogue illustrating the persuasive methods.

How Attitudes Are Formed and Protected

Psychologists say our attitudes are influenced by the way we see the world around us, and conversely our perception of the world is influenced by the attitudes we hold. As infants, we first perceived the world and then acquired attitudes. Throughout the formative years, however, these attitudes influence further perception and attitude formation. We start life with a clean slate, but each of our attitudes in later life is shaped by those we already hold.

We acquire attitudes first through family influence and later through the church and school. During adolescence, we tend to be influenced more by peers (friends and associates our own age) and peer groups (formal or informal clubs, clusters of friends or cliques) and less by our families. In early childhood, the family satisfies virtually all our needs for love, attention, approval, and security, but as we grow older more and more of these needs are met by our peers. In times of stress or crisis, we may return to the family for support, though even this impulse diminishes with the passage of time. With maturity comes a heightened self-confidence, and spouse or friends usually represent our principal outside sources of strength.

Throughout life, there is a direct relationship between our needs and the attitudes we develop. In childhood, accepting the attitudes of our parents is one way to gain their approval; so our earliest feelings about religion and politics usually reflect the beliefs of our parents. Later, in school or church, we encounter information or attitudes that appear to contradict what we learned at home. We return to our family for help in sorting out the "truth." Eventually, however, this sorting function shifts to peers.

As college students, we form new friendships (peer groups). Psychologists suggest that we seek friends whose attitudes toward life are like our own and who share our point of view .They cushion the emotional impact for us when our attitudes are challenged.

As adults, of course, we ordinarily hold "memberships" in several peer groups simultaneously. But the attitudes of these groups also tend to complement and reinforce one another. The members share our feelings about politics, race, sex, and how to have a good time. They provide us with the consistent outlook we need to order our world. To preserve this consistency, we protect our attitudes from conflicting pressures. One of the ways we protect them is by putting on custom-made "blinders" when we examine new information—a process known as *selectivity*.

Selectivity, essentially, is our tendency to choose carefully which aspects of our environment we will permit ourselves to (1) see; (2) accept without distortion; and (3) remember. In other words, when exposed to a new set of "facts" we are likely to screen out whatever contradicts our entrenched attitudes and beliefs—whatever we do not wish to see.

Suppose, for instance, that your family has impressed upon you since childhood that no one gets anything for nothing, that it is everybody's obligation to "make something of himself," that it is sinful to be jobless, and that to "go on the county" is to shame and humiliate your family. In school, you are studying the welfare system in your social problems class. You learn there are many unemployed people who haven't "made something of themselves" (in your parents' terms), and who regularly depend on welfare checks. Are these people seeking something for nothing? According to your teacher, many of them would like to get jobs, but the present welfare arrangement actually discourages this because the payments are reduced by the amount that the person earns. For example, if a widow with five children got a job teaching school, she might be earning a bit more than her welfare payments provided. But her expenses would include transportation to her job and someone to care for any children not yet in school; so she might have less money in the long run to buy food and clothing for her family and pay the rent. Your teacher's point is that welfare should *supplement* the income of a poor person, so that person can have the dignity of a job and also enjoy a decent standard of living.

All this information is brand new to you, and since you identify quite strongly with your parents' belief that anyone on welfare is automatically lazy and irresponsible, you will protect that belief. One mental trick you might use is to avoid hearing the message: as soon as you hear the teacher defending those on welfare, you stop listening and start to daydream. Another is to balance the message with a "fact" of your own that seems to contradict it: the teacher says that a poor person with a low-paying job might still need welfare to buy clothes for his family (you recall that your church distributes used clothing to the needy). The teacher mentions the desire of many people on welfare to have jobs (you recall that she was once a social worker and naturally she would be sympathetic toward those on welfare). If you can't avoid or counteract the message, you will probably forget it as soon as you walk out of the classroom. You are shaking off a set of facts without examining them thoroughly because they do not coincide with your view of reality—something most people do all the time. Because the attitudes coloring their outlooks are different, no two people have the same view of reality; and our views often conflict with those of others. (More about this in the final chapter.)

Instilling, Reinforcing, or Changing an Attitude

You often encounter arguments on subjects you know nothing about. Sometimes, however, you know something about a subject, but you haven't yet formed an attitude or opinion about it. You may hear a speaker making a plea for United Nations intervention in a civil war raging between African nations. This information is new to you; you hold no attitude about the war as yet. If the speaker wants the fighting stopped, he must provide you with facts about the situation, then help you shape an attitude about it before he can expect you to take action. To instill an attitude, the speaker attempts to tie the new attitude to an already existing one. Before asking you to petition the U.N., the practiced persuader may first appeal to negative attitudes toward all wars or to negative attitudes toward human suffering.

The easiest task facing any persuader is reinforcing an existing attitude. Most human beings have favorable attitudes toward many subjects. These range from abstract notions such as truth, justice, and brotherhood, to concrete things like cars, home, and friends. We also tend to have unfavorable attitudes toward things like rape, murder, death, sickness, and violence. Some attitudes are more intense than others. Your attitudes toward your family or home are probably more intense than those you hold toward your car. Your attitudes toward death are more intense than your attitudes about sickness. In analyzing his audience, the speaker must understand the intensity as well as the direction of the attitudes they hold.

Changing another's attitude is the most difficult task, because the ways we shape and protect our attitudes tend to keep us from seeing the wisdom of another's position—man is not the rational animal he is often made out to be. Students often think their persuasion has failed because they couldn't present their material "logically" enough. If this were so, one would only have to master logic and reasoning to be a successful persuader, but this is not enough. True, trained debaters "win" debates through argumentation and reasoning. But the winners are chosen by judges trained to evaluate the logic for its own sake. This kind of argument would have little effect in the everyday world, because most people do not appreciate logic as such. Frequently, they refuse even to "hear" arguments contrary to theirs. If you seek to change the opinion of another, you will need more than logic to convince him that you are right and he is wrong.

Three Persuasive Techniques

In order to instill or alter the attitudes of an audience, persuasive speakers usually rely on one or more of three principal factors, described in detail below: the impact of their personality, appeals to reason, and appeals to the emotions.

PERSUADING BY PERSONAL IMPRESSION (IMAGE)

The most potent element in persuasion, usually far more important than logic, is the impression or image the listeners have of the speaker. Typically, this impression is based on their perception of his character, reputation, manner, credibility, and authority (or credentials) to speak on the subject. We have all heard the expression "Put your best foot forward, for first impressions are lasting ones." This is certainly true in the persuasive situation. Whatever impression we form of the speaker will have a marked influence on how we react to his commands. If we think he is of good character, his arguments credible, and his manner appealing, we will respond favorably and be more likely to accept his arguments and perhaps even do what he asks. If we feel he is somewhat disreputable, his arguments incredible, and his manner condescending, we will not respond favorably to either his arguments or his commands.

It goes without saying that all of this applies to the writer also. He may have made a good impression on someone when he met him, but that image can change drastically when he expresses himself in a letter to the person. On the basis of the letter alone, he may be judged as sloppy, disorganized, and impatient; or careful, orderly, and discreet. The letter may confirm the impression he made in the conversation, enhance that impression, or destroy it.

As we noted in chapter 3, the term "image" has been badly abused by politicians and admen in recent years. It is precisely because they recognize the importance of image to the buying or voting public that they have taken extreme measures to "doctor" the image of their clients or products. A political candidate may learn to style his hair differently and be coached on how to evade the issues. A new brand of cigarette may be presented as a key to sexual attractiveness. In both cases, the idea is to make the "product" seem more valuable, exciting, and useful than it really is.

By contrast, no one objects to a person trying to improve himself by reading more, taking voice lessons, studying public speaking, or enrolling in sensitivity training. All these efforts reflect a sincere desire to become a better person—not an attempt to mislead the public. The impression your audience has of you will reflect the kind of person your training and experience has made you. Approach the job of improving your personal image with a genuine intention of expanding your knowledge, improving your communicative skills, and broadening your understanding of your fellow man, and no one can fault you. But avoid the temptation to deceive your audience, since the results could be disastrous. The impact you will have upon the members of your audience is difficult to predict in any case. All any speaker of integrity can do to enhance his image is to be himself.

It is ironic that this most potent element of persuasion is so hard to measure and identify in actual practice. Psychologists agree that factors like character, manner, credibility, and authority together play an important role in the impressions we form of another, though they do not single out any one characteristic as *the* most important. They also agree that certain attributes will have more appeal for certain types of people than for others. Generally, audiences find it easier to identify with speakers who resemble them in terms of values and personal goals. The most successful speaker often seems to be one who exemplifies not only what we are, but also all that we *would like to be*. In other words, he is a living ideal of our hopes, values, and way of life. From there it is but a short step for him to become our idol.

PERSUADING WITH REASON

Unlike image or appeals to the emotions, which tend to by-pass man's rational processes, reasoning is the element of persuasion that is directed toward his brain. The speaker commonly begins with a bit of evidence—the cost of going to college is getting higher every day; and reasons his way to a conclusion—the government will have to provide more unrestricted funds for higher education. If his evidence is valid and his reasoning sound, hopefully his listener will reach the same conclusion. What is valid evidence? It can be either fact or opinion. Facts are things we can measure or test, such as the price of tuition or the speed of a car. Any audience member looking at your fact would have to identify it in the same way you did—"yes, tuition fees are very high."

As a listener, your problem in verifying facts is that you have neither the time, opportunity, or know-how to check all the information you are bombarded with. Consequently, you will accept some facts at face value, simply because you respect the person who gives you those facts. But in other cases, you'd like some way to evaluate the evidence you're hearing. The tests that follow may be of some use; you can also use them to check the validity of your own facts when you speak.

1. Did the speaker observe his facts firsthand, or is he passing along what someone else has told him? Hearsay evidence isn't admissible in court, and it shouldn't be acceptable to you either.

2. Is it likely that he observed the things he is reporting? If your classmate tells you that he saw the President of the United States drinking heavily at many social functions, you would do well to question his credibility.

3. Is he giving you all the facts? What if someone tells you his car gets thirty miles to the gallon even though it is a V-8? Follow-up cross-examination might reveal that this happened only once when his odometer was out of whack.

4. Is what he is telling you consistent with what you already know? The speaker who says that anyone who criticizes the government is un-American suggests that members of any opposing political party are un-American. This is hardly consistent with the philosophy behind a democracy as you think of it.

5. Can he *prove* his reporting is factual? The quickest way to the truth is to ask for proof.

Opinion as evidence. Some information cannot serve as factual evidence; it is opinion and nothing more. But all opinion is not worthless. Neither is all opinion of equal value. If you offer your opinion about how to curb inflation it will be taken less seriously than that of a qualified economist because you lack his education and experience. You would trust a trained auto mechanic who says your spark plugs need pulling and replacing. But if he tells you your aching tooth needs to be pulled, you might thank him for his concern but leave the decision to your dentist.

The best way to support your conclusions is by citing the conclusions of experts who agree with you. Their prestige and authority lends credibility to your opinion. But two problems often arise when we look for expert opinion to bolster our arguments. First, we often find that experts do not agree with each other. Second, audiences are not always familiar with recognized experts in a particular field. In the latter case, you will need to convince your audience that your expert *is* an expert. When you quote an authority, be sure he is highly regarded in the area in which you quote him. Experts often have opinions on matters not related to their specialities. In those situations they may have no more expertise than any layman.

As there are tests to determine the validity of facts, so there are tests to check the validity of opinion. You can apply these tests to speakers who are quoting the experts or you can try them yourself.

1. Is the authority clearly identified? If you are citing a specific fact, you must give the name of a *particular* authority to support it. More general contentions, widely accepted by experts in the field for a number of years, may be stated as fact without naming a particular source.

2. Is this authority qualified in terms of:

   a. Training—is he an expert in the field your speech is treating? Cite the opinions of doctors on medical topics and the opinion of auto mechanics in matters of engines.

   b. Experience—the opinion of a recent law school graduate wouldn't carry as much weight as that of the law school dean or of famous attorneys like F. Lee Bailey or Melvin Belli.

3. Is the expert concealing hidden biases that might effect the validity of his opinion? The garage owner who recommends a particular brand of oil may do so because he sells it or because an oil company subsidizes his race car.

4. Is the speech lopsided? An argument that overemphasizes opinion rather than facts, or the views of one expert only, is suspect. It suggests that the speaker hasn't done his homework or is purposely withholding information. Combine fact and opinion when presenting your evidence. If you find that there seems to be only one author writing on your topic, consult the librarian; you may have overlooked another source.

Putting the evidence together. Common sense suggests that people are persuaded as much by the way evidence is put together as by the evidence itself. We've all listened to speakers, for example, who *seem* to know what they're talking about. They toss out a fact here, an opinion there, and the name of an expert or two along the way. But listening to these individuals is a frustrating experience. We have to do more than our share as the audience, because *we* have to put these pieces together. In these situations the speaker will find it impossible to *persuade* us because we are working so hard at simply *understanding* him.

The wise speaker, on the other hand, knows that his effectiveness depends on the structure he provides for his material. His credentials as an organizer are at stake. He can choose one or more of the methods of organization discussed earlier (see pp. 125–127), depending on his topic and audience. But the main point is that he must choose *some* organizational pattern.

In all honesty, however, finding the best organizational pattern for your speech may not be as simple as it sounds. This is because the persuasive speaker (or writer) must know when to emphasize and reemphasize points he has made and at the same time bring in key facts and opinion to move his audience. Suppose for example that you are giving a talk on the merits of apartment living. You have a striking fact (apartment living means no lawn-mowing or snow-shoveling) and an expert opinion (housing authority E. Baltzell believes apartment living is cheaper). When do you bring these points into your talk? Not as you begin, certainly, since that will result in a letdown later. The right moment to introduce these facts will depend on your audience. Let's say it is a group of younger people. The economic benefit of cheaper living will appeal to them, but the point of greater free time (no lawn-mowing or snow-shoveling) will be even more significant. Knowing the audience as you do, your best approach might be to start with a general explanation of the problem everyone faces in finding a suitable dwelling. From there you might move into an economic comparison of home ownership versus apartment renting. A good starting point could be your expert's opinion. The final portion of the talk would probably be your discussion of the free-time advantages in apartment living; and you would want to save your punchline about lawn-mowing and snow-shoveling till the very end. It's a point everyone can identify and agree with.

Oversimplified as this organization plan is, it nevertheless points out the importance of structuring your talk carefully. The good persuasive speaker, in sum, is both explainer and strategist. He gets across ideas that are both understood and accepted.

The third important element in persuasion is the speaker's appeal to the audience's emotions. We have all experienced the kind of gut-level reactions loaded words like "nigger," "bastard," "commie," "Fascist" evoke from us. At the other end of the emotional scale, words like "darling" and "baby" evoke certain *physical* responses. What is happening? Is the body playing tricks on us? Not at all. Strong emotions generate similar physical reactions—heightened pulse rate, faster breathing, pounding heart and moist palms—but there is an intellectual facet to any emotion as well. The brain decides what physical activity would be an appropriate response to the stimulus causing the emotional reaction. If we found ourselves being attacked by a gang of hoods, the appropriate activity might be to run, and we would label the emotion fear. Or if only one person were attacking us, the appropriate response might be counterattack and the emotion would be recognized as rage. Or, should someone you care about show a lot of consideration for your feelings, your reaction might be labeled love; but the physical symptoms would be no different than in the previous examples.

The fact that emotions play such a large role in shaping our behavior is important to the persuader, because in certain communication situations—requiring an immediate positive response from the audience—appeals to the emotions get the job done faster than reasoned persuasion or personal appeal. Professional advertisers know the power of the emotional appeal. The next time you watch TV count the number of times emotional appeals occur in car, aftershave, and hair-tonic ads.

Such appeals are successful persuaders because of the triangular relationship between attitudes, motives, and emotions. The attitudes we hold have their roots in our emotions—they satisfy our needs and desires. Emotions in turn reflect the intensity of those attitudes. To change another's attitudes, the persuader tries to determine the emotional strength of the attitude and the desires it satisfies. He then manipulates the listener by appealing to the emotions and motives underlying that attitude.

There is an acknowledged distinction between inborn motives and those we acquire after birth. The former relate to basic physical needs, the latter to social needs. The former include self-preservation, thirst, hunger, sex, and freedom from restraint. The latter include prestige, approval, and affection. These are not all-inclusive lists. Social motives, especially, are not separate and distinct; they tend to operate in combination with one another. There is a danger in assuming that either attitudes or motives can be easily identified by the layman. Trained psychologists find it difficult to explain the causes of human behavior, and warn against making snap judgments about people.

In conversational communication, the motives that shape a person's attitudes can often be determined by direct questioning. A simple "why do you feel that way?" may provide you with the answer you seek. As the conversation progresses, your antagonist may reveal other, deeper motives for the way he feels, and you can adjust your strategy accordingly. For example, suppose you are trying to convince a friend to vote for a woman who is running for mayor. At first your friend insists that the candidate isn't qualified, but when you point out her excellent record as a member of the city council he shifts his argument, claiming that "women don't belong in city government." Obviously, your strategy would have to be revised to deal with this more basic, less rational, motive.

In any persuasive encounter, formal or informal, it is wise to have some loosely structured strategy in mind before you begin. The next section provides you with several.

Persuasive Strategies

The only difference between the trained persuader and the amateur is a difference in readiness—the trained persuader knows what he is setting out to do and how he will do it. He has a plan or strategy he applies to the persuasive situation. The five essential steps of any such strategy have been isolated and defined by Alan H. Monroe,[1] in an arrangement that has come to be known as Monroe's motivated sequence: attention, need,

1. For the material on the motivated sequence, we are indebted to Alan H. Monroe's *Principles and Types of Speech* (Chicago, 1962), chapters 16 and 17.

satisfaction, visualization, and action. Let's follow the sequence from start to finish, and see how it works.

Attention. All communicative acts, oral or written, formal or informal, begin with an attempt to capture the receiver's attention. If you don't have that, communication can't take place. (Any of the introductory techniques suggested in the chapter on the informative message would suit your purposes in the persuasive message as well.) Your primary concern in the initial moments of your presentation is to concentrate the receiver's attention on you and your message.

Need. In this step, your objective is to create a need in your listener for your product or belief. While this is normally accomplished by pointing up the benefits of a change (for example, "Trade up to a new model"), you might also suggest the benefits of avoiding change (for example, "Let's picket the local brewery—they want to raise beer prices and we need to keep it within reach of students and people on fixed incomes"). This step can help develop a new attitude (for example, "Let's work now to protect the moon from becoming a refuse heap"). You would probably expand each of these three propositions, as suggested below, to make sure you had established the need in question.

"Trading up to a new model" involves modifying thought and action. You might address your audience like this: "Had any big repair bills to pay on your old machine lately? Any more coming up in the near future? Getting tired of sinking more money into your car while it steadily depreciates? Remember, it will never be worth more than it is worth right now!"

The speaker attempting to freeze the price of beer wants to reinforce an attitude, and he might proceed like this: "Ever notice how as prices go up, up, up, and wages and salaries of organized laborers and executives go up, wages of students like you and me stay the same? Not only have food prices increased, but the price of that one item contributing more to our leisure-time enjoyment than any other is also going to be raised. Brothers and sisters, I'm talking about the price of BEER! If the price goes up, as announced by the breweries, people on fixed incomes will have to settle for less enjoyment."

The speaker concerned about the moon wants to instill an attitude, which he might try to do like this: "Ever driven through a big city and been disgusted by the filth on sidewalks? The haze in the air bother you? How about the smell? Or the slums? The unsightly tangle of billboards and dilapidated factories? Ever wonder how people let it get that way? For that matter, have you driven out in the country lately? Do you like the rusting discarded implements lying in the fields? Or the junked cars? Ever wonder if anybody cares? If they're ever going to do something about it? Did you follow the Apollo missions on TV? Notice how much stuff they left behind? How much they jettisoned? Ever wonder how much junk future moon landings will leave behind? Ever hear about anybody making plans to clean it up?

Satisfaction. The satisfaction step logically picks up where the need step left off. Here, you demonstrate how your proposal will satisfy the needs you have just outlined. The attention and need steps parallel the introduction to the speech—they attract, focus, and heighten the audience's interest in your topic. In the satisfaction step, you develop the body of the speech. (Any of the forms of development discussed in the previous chapter are applicable to persuasive communication as well.)

Visualization. In the fourth step of the motivated sequence, you will round out the body of the speech by helping your audience to visualize or "see" benefits they will derive from accepting your proposal, product, or belief. The hypothetical illustration, for example, can be used to paint a word picture of conditions that will improve should your plan be accepted. For example, the student urging his friends to demonstrate against the proposed increase in the price of beer might use this hypothetical illustration: "Picture yourself in the Beer and Brat with the rest of the gang. The music is nice, and your friends are happy. There are eight at your table and the beer is going down smooth. Someone buys the first round, someone else another, then it's your turn. You order eight more and when the waiter comes back with the beer, the check totals only $4. That's right, gang! Fifty cents a beer, not sixty or seventy-five, but fifty! That's entertainment anyone can afford!"

Visual aids such as slides or sketches can also be used to illustrate your point, particularly if other people have already put your plan into operation at some other place. For example, if you are proposing a shopping mall in your town, help your audience visualize such a mall by showing pictures of towns that already have one. A well-done sketch can serve the same purpose. These visual aids work best with speeches proposing tangible things. However, intangibles such as increased beer costs can be illustrated with figures on a chalk board, poker chips, or slips of paper to represent dollar bills. Set your imagination free. You will be surprised at what commonplace things you can use to symbolize even the most abstract concepts.

Action. The close of the persuasive speech is designed to clinch the objective of the speech as you defined it in your specific purpose. This step spells out what attitudes you want your receivers to accept, strengthen, or change or what new course of action you want them to follow. The speaker urging you to demonstrate against the beer price increase or help put a stop to the moon littering doesn't just want to convince you that something ought to be done—he wants you to *do something!* He might pass around a petition that would be sent to the president of the brewery in the one case or your U.S. senators or congressmen in the other. He wouldn't suggest that you write the appropriate officials "when you get home from the meeting"; he'd do as much of the work as possible himself beforehand to be assured of maximum results.

Application of Persuasive Theory

To pull all this theoretical material together let's apply it to a typical persuasive communication situation you might encounter at school. Let's assume you are sitting at a table in the student Union having a cup of coffee with two of your friends before going to your next class. These friends, Fred Jones and Tom Carter, are about your age. They live downtown near the campus while you live in a suburb with your parents.

While you are sitting there in walks Art Cooper growling about the traffic he had to fight to get downtown to school from the house he rents in the suburbs. Art, a data processing student, is being sent to school by his employer, a suburban branch bank near his home. Today he is launching into his favorite topic: "The city needs an expressway system to rid itself of the miserable traffic conditions during rush hours." You and your friends have heard Art on this subject many times. You know almost by heart the direction his tirade will take: "The city isn't progressive enough, it's afraid of losing a few buildings, the city could stand to get rid of some of the slums in its inner core, city fathers don't know what they are talking about," and so on.

As you listen to Art you glance at the faces of your friends. As you anticipated, they are amused most of the time, but when Art hits a point contrary to their attitudes a flicker of irritation crosses their faces. Fred, for example, has a love for the historic old mansions that dot the downtown sector. When Art dismisses them as "old relics" Fred gets rather annoyed. He feels that to destroy these landmark mansions for the sake of moving more traffic into the downtown area would be criminal. Tom is not particularly concerned about architecture, but he doesn't appreciate Art's overlooking the importance of a few parks in the downtown neighborhoods. Living there himself, he finds the lush green of the park a welcome relief from the soot and grime of the concrete canyons. To replace parks with concrete "spaghetti" (expressways) would make his neighborhood uglier still.

You consider the situation at hand. You think that everyone's interests would be best served by a mass transit system. Fred and Tom don't seem to have strong feelings on the subject either way, so you could probably instill favorable attitudes in them without much trouble. The real target is Art, who has made it clear before that he considers mass transit a lost cause—too expensive and time-consuming to install. You realize from previous conversations with Art that he has been arguing from his heart rather than his head, blindly refusing to see things in any different light than his own. His attitude will be difficult to change.

Though your arguments have failed before, you think you have a good chance of succeeding now, because you have prepared yourself in advance for a change. You have done home-work on the idea of a mass transit system, and you think you can convince Fred and Tom and Art. On the basis of what you have heard and read, you think mass transit wouldn't require the removal of historic landmarks (a point to stress for Fred's sake), wouldn't remove a blade of park grass (a point to stress for Tom's sake), and would enhance—not detract from—the beauty of the skyline (a point Tom and Fred would appreciate). More importantly, you think mass transit is cheaper than ex-pressways; and it would take no more time to install a monorail or subway than to build a new road. It would also be fairer to downtown residents and healthier for everyone. These last points will be what you emphasize most, since they are directed at Art.

You begin your argument. As you do, so you keep in mind the motivated sequence technique for persuasion. You also re-member that Art's attitudes are based on needs which you must prove you can satisfy, if you are to change those attitudes.

YOU (attention step): Art, you make it sound as if you were the only one with the problem of getting downtown during rush hour. Practically all of us have the same problem. Yet there's a simpler way of solving it than building an expensive freeway system right through the heart of downtown, a way it can be done with-out tearing down so many of the historical old buildings Fred *opinion* here is in favor of saving. I'll also bet it can be done without sacrificing any of the few remaining parks. In fact, I'll bet it can be done in a way that would be cheaper initially *and* in the long run. And it wouldn't uproot people or contribute as much to air pollution as expressways would.

ART: You aren't going to give me that mass transit stuff again, are you? I've told you before you aren't going to sell that to my neighbors. We've heard all that before and it doesn't cut any more ice now than it did then!

YOU (attention step): Well, just listen a minute, Art. As you drive into town every day do you ever notice how many of the cars are carrying only one person? I have. It's a little game I play while I wait for the bus. I've been counting for a few weeks *fact* now, and between 70 and 80% of the cars that drive past the bus stop have only one person in the car.

I've noticed something else rather interesting too. Most of the time I ride the bus, as I've said. But occasionally I get a ride with somebody from school. And you know something? You're all cursing each other. The bus driver is cursing the car drivers, and the drivers of the cars I've ridden in are cursing the buses.

appeal to mental stability

opinion ART: Why not? They hog the road—turn out in front of you. If it weren't for them a guy could make better time.

YOU: Right! But did you ever stop to think you all are trying to do the same thing at the same time and you're just getting in each other's way?

opinion ART: You're missing the point! If we had eight lanes we would have plenty of room and we wouldn't be getting in each other's way!

YOU *(need step)*: I think you'll find that's so much wishful thinking, Art. Those cities that build expressways find that people still can't get downtown efficiently. That's not too surprising, you know, because we've got all the necessary ingredients—population explosion plus increased number of auto owners and drivers! And given a choice of a good road or a bad one to drive on, people are bound to drive on the good one and that means more traffic on the expressway every year.

opinion

ART: See, you just said yourself that given a better road to drive on people will drive on it; what's going on? You changing your mind after all?

YOU *(need step)*: No, not at all. I won't deny that if we build more expressways more people will drive on them. As I said before that's a well-known fact. The point is you can't ever build enough expressways to handle all the traffic. Most expressways are obsolete by the time they're completed, and we still have the same need to get downtown quickly and pleasantly. The answer seems to me to lie in some other means for transporting people from one side of town to the other.

opinion based on facts reported by other cities

(Tom and Fred have been trying to break into the conversation at several points, as might be expected. But at this point you are closer to getting Art convinced than ever before, so you politely wave them off.)

YOU *(satisfaction step)*: From what I've been reading lately and what I've seen with my own eyes, I think some type of mass transit is the taxpayer's answer. For example, the average subway train or monorail can hold around 150 people—more in rush hour. Consider the amount of road space taken by that number of individual cars!

appeal to thrift

fact

ART: And that's the catch right there. Where are all those subway or monorail cars going to come from? How can the city pay for them and what would we do with them during the nonpeak-load periods? The city can't make its bus system self-supporting now as it is, and if we put in a subway or monorail, the costs go still higher and we get deeper in the red yet!

fact/opinion

YOU *(satisfaction step)*: That's a legitimate argument, Art. Nobody has yet come up with a system that will be cheaper than what we now have. But if 99% of the commuters—businessmen, shoppers, students, factory workers—rode the monorail, instead of the 5% that ride the buses, it would be self-supporting in a relatively short time. A high-speed monorail is a lot more attractive to most commuters than a bus that stops at every other corner—OR a car stalled in a massive traffic jam.

fact/appeal to thrift

opinion

I think we've got to accept the fact that whatever the solution is, it's going to cost money. The question is which solution will cost us less in the long run—and not just in the economic sense alone.

FRED: Well, I'll buy the mass transit idea for no other reason than it saves a few of the old mansions downtown. They just don't make 'em like that anymore!

TOM: You know, Art, it would be nice of you suburban guys to leave us *one* park downtown anyway!

ART: Parks and mansions! I'm amazed at you guys. That's all you think of.

TOM: Yourself and your car; that's all *you* ever think of! And I'm not amazed.

YOU: They've got a point, Art. After all, we all want our cities to be more than just buildings and roadways. We ought to make them enjoyable places to live and raise a family. You ought to be able to stroll through them on Sunday afternoon and hear the

appeal to individual and family well-being

birds sing in the trees. I also see your point about taxes, though, and I'd like to mention another point we've overlooked. You know, when you put in an expressway system, you wipe out industrial buildings which help pay those taxes for the downtown areas. This means when those buildings go, your tax bill increases to pay for downtown services.

appeal to thrift

ART: Yeah, but if we got rid of the slums downtown, we wouldn't have to pay so much anyway.

YOU: *(satisfaction step)*: That's another issue, really. All downtown areas aren't slums. Tom and Fred here aren't slum residents by any means. They like living where they are, but they want the same things we do in the suburbs. They want to be able to relax in well-maintained parks. They want to preserve a little architectural charm from the past. After work they want to step outside on the porch and inhale fresh air. Incidentally, have you ever stopped to think how much air pollution the modern car contributes? More expressways mean more cars, and that means more air pollution. That means bad air for all of us, downtown and in the suburbs too.

ppeal to ood health

ART: Okay, I can see the point about that. But you're ducking the issue about slums.

YOU *(satisfaction and visualization steps)*: Well, maybe I just didn't make it clear. What I'm saying is three things. One is that you don't get rid of slums by just tearing them down. The people who lived there will have to find other inexpensive apartments, and if the city doesn't provide decent public housing we'll just have the same problem all over again, somewhere else.

appeal to sense of shelter

Second, it's not just the slums that will go; some people with nice homes in the suburbs will have to give them up, and they don't do that without a lot of regrets and bad feeling. How would you like it if someone wanted to run a superhighway right through your living room? Also, the city will have to buy those homes at top market prices, and that can get expensive when you're talking about a hundred or so homes.

appeal to civic unity

Third, we shouldn't be thinking of suburban problems and downtown problems as two separate, unrelated things. Mass transit would enable suburbanites to zip to and from work without getting tired and short-tempered in the traffic—and incidentally without being involved in the accidents that often occur on busy expressways. At the same time, it would enable the city to renovate the downtown area without permanently dislocating people.

Picture yourself out in the backyard tonight, weeding the garden. You got home quickly and more pleasantly by mass transit. The air is cleaner because of the fewer cars. You've got a little more money in your pocket because the city voted mass transit instead of an expensive expressway system.

Think of how much more satisfying all this is to you if you know that some guy downtown is happy too. He's got his architectural landmarks and parks. His air is cleaner, and he hasn't been forced to move. He's as glad that his kids have a nice place to live as you are. The whole city—downtown and suburb alike—gives you a good feeling.

ART: Mmn. Maybe. Look, I've got a class to go to now, but I'd like to talk to you about this some more.

YOU *(action step)*: I'd like that too. How about meeting me here Tuesday, same time? And I've been reading an interesting book on this subject you might like to see. I'll bring it along if you want.

ART: Sure, why not? See you then.

Summary

In this chapter we have defined persuasion as the deliberate attempt to instill, reinforce, or change attitudes or behavior by means of personal impression (image), reason, and appeals to the emotions. We saw that attitudes are first formed at home and later influenced by our membership in peer groups. Once formed, they are protected by continued identification with the family and the peer group, as well as the process of selectivity.

Three elements of persuasion were identified: the personal impression the sender makes, the reasoning ability he employs, and his appeals to the emotions of his audience. Personal impression is derived from his character, mannerisms, and credibility. Reasoning involves the ability to put evidence together in an appeal to man's sense of logic. Appealing to the emotions involves a sender provoking laughter, tears, anger, and so on in his audience.

Assignments

1. Form discussion groups with the intent of determining hidden motives for the attitudes each of you holds on a currently controversial issue.

2. As a class, analyze a major televised political address or live speech given in your community. At the next class meeting split into three discussion groups treating the following topics: (1) the speaker's image, (2) his ability to reason, (3) the appeals he made to his audience's emotions and motives.

3. Construct a questionnaire that would reveal your classmates' attitudes about a topic of concern in your community. Possible topics might include: candidates running for political office in your town, pollution problems faced by local industries, abortion, and so on.

4. Prepare a short (three-page) paper discussing situations where the three persuasive elements (personal impression, reason, appeals to the emotions) might best be used.

5. Go out into your local business community and observe the persuasive selling efforts used by salesmen in three different types of stores. Write a short paper describing the efforts they made to relate their persuasive methods to their customers.

9

The Persuasive Message in Written Communication

JUST AS WE applied the material on informative spoken messages to written communications, we will now do the same with the persuasive message. But before we do that let us add one final note about persuasion in general. It may clear up some lingering confusion.

When we speak of "persuasion" we are not using the term in a negative sense. We do not mean manipulation with intent to use the listener or reader for selfish or unethical ends. In essence, then, we are saying that persuasion in no way implies trickery or gimmickry. Yet the persuasive message is necessary because there are times when we want to bring others around to our way of thinking or reinforce a previous attitude. On these occasions we need to approach the situation differently than if we were merely informing them of something.

Nor, as we have already noted, are the differences between information and persuasion all that great. The informative sender who can muster his facts in an orderly fashion is often as persuasive as the sender who sets out to persuade in the first place. The informative letter that gets directly to the point carries as much weight in the receiver's mind as the persuasive letter that opens with a flow of purple prose.

With these thoughts in mind suppose we turn now to some practical applications of written persuasive messages: first, four kinds of business letters, followed by several off-the-job items. We begin with the letter of complaint.

Letters of Complaint

Some people have the notion that letters of complaint are meant solely for "sounding off." That may indeed relieve some of the anger and frustration for the sender, but it results in anything but a good written persuasive message. This is because sounding off rarely accomplishes a specific change in the thinking or action of the receiver. Rather it alienates the receiver by placing him immediately on the defensive. His reaction is to hold his ground rather than reconsider. His first impulse is to counterattack.

The intelligent sender of a complaint letter knows better

than to use this technique. Instead he uses a fairly standard pattern: first, he communicates the specific problem, let us say the breakdown of a walkie-talkie he ordered through a mail-order house; second, he communicates the background circumstances involving the product's breakdown, that is, what part is not working; third, he provides some possible excuse for the company without detracting from the fact that he deserves compensation (a case of shipping damage, say); finally he states specifically what that remedy should be, in this case repair or replacement. The letter in Figure 8 follows this general pattern.

Notice how this letter conforms to a problem-solving pattern. The specific problem is the effect of receiving a broken walkie-talkie on Tom Jesperson. The possible solutions are the replacement or repair of the broken item. And the conclusion is a request for the company to take direct action.

Apart from this problem-solving pattern, however, notice how effective this letter is in terms of the receiver's reaction. It gets to the point right away, it supplements the main point with needed information, it tells the receiver what he might do to pacify the customer.

The third paragraph is persuasive because the sender genuinely tries to see the receiver's possible difficulties. The sender tries to empathize—to use a term from chapter 3—with the receiver. When this occurs, the receiver is much more likely to see the sender's point of view too.

It should be emphasized here that this procedure is suitable only for the initial letter of complaint. Needless to say, if the sender keeps on sending letters and getting no action, then the persuasion becomes more forceful and the letters shorter. For example, someone who wants to get paid for his services and who has had two bills and three letters of complaint ignored by the receiver might send this curt paragraph:

Dear Mr. Brown:
    Unless we receive payment by June 15 for work done on your house in March, we shall begin legal action against you.

```
318 York Road
Oak Brook, Illinois 60532

April 17, 1970

Rand Supply Corporation
14 Britt Parkway
Washington, D. C.  20036

Dear Sirs:

In this morning's mail I received a walkie-talkie
I had ordered from your company.  You can imagine
how disappointed I felt at finding it broken and
unworkable.

The walkie-talkie is the model I ordered on
March 19.  But this particular walkie-talkie has
something loose internally so the sound trans-
mission cuts out after a person speaks into it.
Not being an engineer I can't deduce exactly what
is wrong.  I can only tell you that it's impossible
to say more than three words into it without losing the
transmission.

I'd like to think that this defect might not be
your fault, that somehow your product got damaged in
being mailed to me.  We all know how delicately
engineered items get maltreated in transit these days.

(continued..)
```

Figure 8.   Sample Letter of Complaint

Nevertheless, I have to insist that I receive
quality merchandise from your firm. Therefore I'm
sending the walkie-talkie back to you so that you
can replace it or repair it. Of these two courses
of action I would prefer that you replace the
product entirely, but if an adequate repair job
will make the product like new, then that will be
acceptable.

I look forward to your prompt attention to this
matter.

Sincerely yours,

Tom Jesperson

Figure 8.   Sample Letter of Complaint (*cont.*)

Fortunately, most people react favorably to initial letters of complaint if they are appropriately written. Thus persuasion seldom reaches this extreme.

Letters that Answer Complaint Letters

The persuasive message also applies in written responses to complaint letters. In most business and industrial situations, however, sending such a letter may not be advisable if a phone is handy; calling someone immediately to answer his complaint gives you a psychological advantage in soothing him. The fact that you called him personally indicates your genuine concern for his problem. This rule will not apply in all cases—the tone of the complaint letter might indicate that the complaining person will just fly off the handle if he gets you on the line—but in most cases it is valid.

Assume for the moment, however, that you cannot phone for some reason or that calling is inadvisable. In that case, how do you structure a letter that answers a complaint letter? Most top-notch persuasive letter writers begin by restating in their own words the complaint of the original letter. This would be a good persuasive strategy for you to use, because it makes the receiver, the complainer, feel that he has at least been understood. After that, you tell the complainer how you will remedy the situation, if at all. If there is no remedy, then you must use very delicate though frank persuasion to convince the complainer that your position is a just one. Here is where empathy enters the picture once more; you must try to get the complainer to see your side of the story. Finally, you leave the door open for further discussion on the matter. This lets the complainer know once more that he is dealing with reasonable human beings, that if he is still not satisfied the matter is not closed entirely. Figure 9 illustrates a letter that meets all the foregoing requirements fairly well.

Notice once more how this letter conforms to the well-organized problem-solving approach, but notice above all how the sender has managed to get the complainer to see things his way.

R⊕SS

EXTERMINATORS

4453 W. Lawnside Ave. / Newton, Fla. 03243

February 19, 1969

Mrs. Ruth Whitman
9 Chesapeake Bay Drive
Newton, Florida 13610

Dear Mrs. Whitman:

I have just read your letter asking for a reduction in our bill for the exterminating work we
did for you in January. As I understand it, you are
asking for a reduction in the overtime amount we
charged for Saturday, January 15.

Before I get to the specific problem let me
say how glad I was to hear from you. Any businessman knows how valuable it is to receive direct
complaints from customers rather than via the
grapevine, and we like to hear these complaints to
improve operations.

Now as to your specific problem, I wish I could
offer you a reduction, but I'm afraid I cannot. I
verified the number of hours our crew had worked for you
on Saturday the 15th. I also checked our mathematics
on the bill we sent you. That too was correct.

This leads me to conclude that perhaps you did not
read our contract closely enough. There it states that
any Saturday overtime is billed at double time, not
time and a half. Could this be the source of our
difficulty? The foreman of our crew thought you understood this billing rate before we proceeded with our
Saturday work, but perhaps this was not the case. If
that is true, then we are remiss in not pointing this out
to you adequately. At the same time, however, we have
to assume that our customers read their contracts carefully.

(continued...)

Figure 9.   Answer to Complaint Letter

As a homeowner myself I can certainly identify with your concern over the costs of keeping up a residence. I've often questioned costs too. At those times, however, I remind myself that quality work is worth paying for.

I hope this answers your specific questions about your bill. If you still have questions by all means call me or write again. And thank you again for bringing this matter to our attention.

Sincerely,

Robert W. Ross

Robert W. Ross

RR:dg

Figure 9.   Answer to Complaint Letter (*cont.*)

He has placed himself in her homeowning shoes and found a common bond between them. He has sandwiched the bad news —no reduction—in the middle of the letter, between two good points. Overall, the tone of the letter is pleasant but firm.

Job Application Letters

A third kind of persuasive letter is the letter of application for a job. Many business and industrial firms consider this kind of letter almost as important as the data sheet it frequently accompanies, because it gives an insight into the applicant's personality and initiative. Ideally it says enough about the applicant's qualifications to make the employer want to read the data sheet, at the same time indicating why the applicant is interested in the job in question—and illustrating his ability to express himself on paper.

The writer's task, then, is to outline his qualifications, with specific reference to the job he is applying for. There are numerous ways to approach this task, but the simplest and most direct is to state the job that you want, and then briefly describe your occupational and educational experience and relevant personal interests (in separate paragraphs).

No matter what approach you use, the important thing is to begin in a dignified way. The use of gimmicks ("If you're looking for an expert draftsman, look no further") and/or a conceited tone may cost you the job before the employer even reads your data sheet. If you have the qualifications the job demands, your credentials will speak for themselves. What you must do is organize your letter logically and concisely, keeping your tone courteous and businesslike throughout, so the employer will conclude not only that you seem qualified, but also that you are the kind of person he would like to have on his staff.

One ticklish item concerns salary. In general, unless you are answering an ad that specifically asks you to indicate your salary requirement, you are better off saying nothing about it. If the employer decides he wants to hire you, he will make you an offer, probably the usual starting salary for the job in question. If you think you deserve more, that is the best moment for you to ask for it. However, if you really want the job, you'd be wise not to ask the firm to raise their offer too much.

The last paragraph in the letter should indicate, as specifically as possible, when you would be available for an interview with the company.

Figure 10 illustrates a letter of application that in all probability would persuade the employer to invite the writer for an interview. Note that, as the writer is applying for an editorial position, she has included samples of her work with the letter and data sheet. The graphics design student we mentioned earlier would certainly bring a portfolio of his work along to any interviews he arranged. By including this material, the applicant provides tangible support (visualization) for the credentials given in the data sheet, and—if his work is of good quality—improves his chances of getting the job.

The structure of this written persuasive message clearly reflects the motivated sequence we described in chapter 8. The first part commands *attention* by referring directly to the *need* that the applicant might fill. The middle explains how the applicant is particularly suited to *satisfy* that need, and the closing calls for the reader to take a significant *action*—contacting the writer. Notice also that the applicant has had a good deal of experience in the field, and has organized her persuasive message around that. In addition, the message is receiver-oriented: designed to help the receiver quickly evaluate the abilities and qualities the applicant would bring to the job.

321 East Maple Ave.
St. Paul, Minnesota 55405

April 30, 1974

Personnel Department
Hoffmann Research Laboratories
212 Central Ave.
Detroit, Michigan 46632

Dear Sirs:

I am writing in reply to your advertisement for a junior computer programmer in the Detroit Times (4/28/74). As indicated on the enclosed data sheet, I will graduate from Arden Community College in June with an A.A. degree in Business Data Processing. At present I am in the upper 25% of my class.

Several of the courses I have taken relate directly to the job your ad describes, in particular Systems for Data Processing I and II, Computer Science I and II, and COBOL Programming I and II. In addition, I completed an independent term project under the supervision of Professor Adam Margolies, setting up and programming a problem in accounts payable subsystems. This experience, I feel, taught me a good deal about problem-oriented programming techniques.

Last summer I worked as an assistant to Dr. Robert Burbank, senior programmer at Corbin Instruments, Inc., in Saginaw, Michigan. Most of my work there involved using the IBM 360 computer to aid Dr. Burbank in writing scientific programs in machine language and Fortran.

(continued...)

Figure 10.   Sample Application Letter

For the past year at Arden, I have served as Vice Chairman of the college business club (Phi Beta Lambda), a job which has included scheduling visiting speakers from area businesses and chairing the question-answer sessions that followed their talks. In addition, I have written a column describing club activities for the Arden <u>Torch</u>.

Should you wish to interview me, I plan to be in Detroit the week of May 14-18, and would be glad to talk with you Monday, May 14, at 1 p.m. If this is inconvenient for you, please contact me at the above address.

I look forward to hearing from you.

Sincerely,

Ellen E. Seibel

Ellen E. Seibel

Enc.: Data sheet

Figure 10. Sample Application Letter (*cont.*)

Sales Letters

The principle of designing your communication with the receiver's viewpoint in mind is extremely critical in the fourth and final kind of persuasive business letter, the sales letter. Everyone has gotten these in the mail at one time or another. They advertise a product or services. They catch your attention because in format they look like a personal letter you would get from a friend —usually the inside address is missing, and sometimes the address in the heading as well.

The organization of this kind of letter varies with the particular product or service, and, of course, with the sender's analysis of the receiver. Some of these letters start with the product's strong point, then proceed to the secondary points, working back to a short clincher paragraph at the end. Others are structured around the needs and desires of the receiver. In these, paragraph one might describe the enjoyment the person could derive from the product—a tennis racket, for instance. The second might deal with the social benefits of playing tennis, i.e., "Look at all the new friends you'll make learning to play the game." A third paragraph might stress the health benefits to be gained from playing. The organization of such letters can be as varied as the possible motives in the receiver.

One particular tip about format (typing arrangement) for the sales letter may be of use here. Instead of indenting the first line of the first paragraph as you normally would, try indenting the last lines, leaving the first two or three longer. These two or three long lines near the beginning then become attention lines, places to put the key selling point, as in the first paragraph of Figure 11.

It will come as no surprise to you that this letter again follows the motivation sequence. The first paragraph gets *attention* immediately. The second establishes a *need* in the receiver's mind. The third and fourth paragraphs show that *need* can be *satisfied*. The fifth gets the receiver to *visualize* himself with those needs satisfied. And the final paragraph calls for some specific *action* on his part. This sales letter is just another example of how the

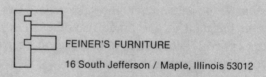

FEINER'S FURNITURE

16 South Jefferson / Maple, Illinois 53012

May 19, 1971

Dear Friend,

Imagine your home or apartment with a whole new look.
A clean, sculptured elegance. A rich appearance.
Impressive. We're talking about a whole new line
of furniture, naturally--the modern line FEINER'S
is offering during its MODERNITY WEEK!

We all know how furniture tends to get dull after a while.
We change, get new and fresh ideas--but the couch, chairs,
and tables stay the same. Something's missing.

That something is the modern look FEINER'S is showing
May 21 to May 29. From New York, Denmark, England--we're
bringing in the latest styles, colors, fabrics, and materials. S-shaped lounge chairs, golf-tee tables, cinnamons,
scarlets, modest teakwoods to rakish steels to practical
plastics. Blow up an easy chair for your party! Deflate
it tomorrow for more space.

All of these items are as functional as they are tasteful.
They're molded to the modern way of life. They're durable.
Yet they're easy on the wallet too.

You can entertain your friends next weekend and show the
new you. Serve cocktails on a chic table from Copenhagen.
Seat your friends on a hip-hugger couch. You can bet
there'll be favorable comments on your contemporary outlook.

(continued...)

Figure 11.   Sample Sales Letter

Make it a point to visit FEINER'S during this important
week. Bring the enclosed invitation and FEINER'S will
give you a $20 discount on all items over $100. We
think the modern look is worth that.

D. R. Lawrence

D. R. Lawrence
for FEINER'S

DL/ba

Figure 11. Sample Sales Letter (*cont.*)

motivation sequence can be applied to on-the-job persuasive messages in writing.

We turn now to the several kinds of written persuasive messages that people construct every day away from their jobs. These include the letter to the editor, the opinion paper, and the review or feature for a club or social group. All have something in common with the other written persuasive messages we have studied.

Letters to the Editor

The letter to the editor of the local newspaper and the opinion paper usually stem from one of these sources: the submission of a bill or resolution by an elected official to a legislative body, the occurrence of an event in the writer's city or town, the presence of a problem in the writer's neighborhood. When such issues are publicized, individual citizens are likely to make their reactions known, often by writing a letter to the local paper. If the letter is a good one, it will be printed on the paper's editorial page. Alternatively, an individual may submit an opinion paper to a club or organization with some interest or influence in the area that concerns him, in hopes of persuading the group as a whole to take a public stand. Or he may be asked by the group to write a paper explaining its views, for public distribution.

In each of these applications, reasoning ideally exceeds use of emotional appeals. The writer brings relevant evidence to bear. He structures the message around arguments that take in his reader's experience—the same approach you encountered in chapter 8, on the spoken persuasive message. In Figure 12, a letter to the editor that would undoubtedly be printed, the writer uses logic and common sense to get her point across.

The appeal throughout the letter is to the reader's common sense, not his emotions. The writer offers three arguments, each well-supported: (1) the attacks are based on misinformation; (2) the would-be censors are inconsistent in trying to set "standards" for the degree of censorship; and (3) by publicizing the book, the censors actually hurt their own cause. The language is not explosive, but deliberate and rational. There is an attempt

213 Elm Street
Langston, Kansas

October 3, 1974

Editor
Langston Herald
101 Center Street
Langston, Kansas

To the Editor:

For the past few weeks I've been following the
controversy over permitting Joseph Heller's
Catch-22 to be taught at Langston High, and I
believe that those parents who have attacked it
as "worthless, pornographic trash" are in error.

To begin with, the few sexual passages in the book
are not intended to shock or excite the reader,
but rather to amplify the book's central message
about the inhuman bureaucracy that rules our
lives in wartime. One cannot help wondering how
many of the protesting parents have actually read
the book from start to finish.

Second, those who argue that use of Catch-22 in
the school is somehow contrary to "community
standards" seem unable to define precisely what
those standards require. At the school board
meeting last week, one parent asserted that the
book should not be discussed in the classroom.
Then, when he learned from the English department
chairman that critics have acclaimed it as a
brilliant work of "black humor," he conceded that
it could remain in the school library--but not
on a class reading list! Others felt the book
should be removed from the school entirely, but
not from the town library--which nearly all
students in the high school belong to.

(continued...)

Figure 12.   Letter to the Editor

Third, few of the protestors seem aware of the
ironic results their activities have produced. The
town library and local bookstores have had to order
many more copies of the book to keep up with the
requests for it, from adults and students alike.
And most younger people who start the book probably
don't even get as far as the episodes that have
caused the fuss. My neighbor's sophomore daughter
came home with the book last Monday. Finding
Heller's prose style way over her head, she had
given up on it by Wednesday.

Those who attempt to limit the choice of material
taught in our schools are, in effect, trying to
limit the education of our students. They do not--
and cannot--speak for the community as a whole.
As professionals, our teachers are best qualified
to select what they shall teach. In overriding the
self-appointed censors, I think the school board has
carried out the public trust and shown that it merits
our full support.

Barbara Smith (Mrs.)

Figure 12.   Letter to the Editor (*cont.*)

to relate to the reader, with references to the school board meeting and the neighbor's daughter; but these references are appeals to his reason, not to his "gut reactions."

Opinion Papers

This particular letter could easily be expanded into an opinion paper. The writer need only add further arguments, or increase her support for the arguments already there, or both. Figure 13 shows how Mrs. Smith reworked her message to represent the views of a group of citizens concerned about the problem.

Given that the protesting parents are too emotionally involved with the *Catch-22* issue to respond to reason, Mrs. Smith's opinion paper will probably have little effect on them. For many of them, their thinking about the book is not really "thinking" at all, as most educated people would define the word.

By the same token, of course, many of those on the opposite side would accept all Mrs. Smith's conclusions without question. They can be as stubborn and inflexible as their opponents—their instant reaction may be that any form of censorship represents "a threat to the freedoms guaranteed by the First Amendment," and nothing could change their minds.

Who, then, is Mrs. Smith writing for? Like the student discussing the virtues of mass transit with his friends, she is trying to reach three groups: those who have never really considered the issue of censorship before; those who still have some doubt about their stand on the issue; and those who, like Art, have made up their minds but are capable of responding favorably to a strong argument for the other side. In light of these three groups, is Mrs. Smith's opinion paper a good one? In some ways yes, in others no—the good points probably outweigh the bad. Her arguments about misinformation and community standards will probably impress all three groups, except that her reference to the Supreme Court is risky—some people tune out on a message as soon as the Court is mentioned. At the same time, however, she could not omit the Court without seriously undermining her argument, since their landmark decision on obscenity is essential to any discussion of that issue. Her argument about

October 17, 1974

To: the Langston School Board, the press, and
    other interested parties

The recent controversy at Langston High School
over classroom use of the novel <u>Catch-22</u> by Joseph
Heller has prompted the formation of a South
Langston Citizens Group, which has investigated
the situation and arrived at some conclusions. Our
position on the <u>Catch-22</u> matter follows.

The attempt by a group of ten parents to remove
the book from the high school, like so many cases
of attempted censorship, is based on little or
no information. Three of the seven protesting
parents who spoke at a recent public meeting at
the school admitted that they had not read the
entire book. The leader of the group, Mrs. Dorothy
Bromley, had read the book completely, yet when
questioned had apparently given no thought to the
author's purpose in writing it. Furthermore, two
of the protestors did not know at what grade
level the book was being taught.

For the record, everyone in our group has read all
of <u>Catch-22</u>. We feel that Heller's intention was
to create a bitter satire on the inhuman bureaucracy that rules our lives during wartime. There
are sexual passages in the book, but we think
the protestors have failed to see the sex in
its proper context. We think, too, that the book
is being taught at the grade level (senior year)
where the realities of war and sex are appropriately investigated.

Figure 13.   Opinion Paper

We are disturbed, then, at the failure of the protesting parents to be fully informed about the book's contents. We are equally disturbed at their use of the term "community standards" in supporting their views at public meetings, implying that the tastes and beliefs of the community as a whole can be measured by the same yardstick.

For all practical purposes "community standards" is a virtually meaningless phrase, as indicated by the actions of the protestors themselves at the school board meeting last week. One said the book should be eliminated from the classroom, but not from the library. Another wanted it removed from both places. One thought Heller's descriptions of sex were tasteless, while another considered them obscene. Clearly, those who oppose the students' use of Catch-22 are anything but unanimous in their feelings about the elusive "community standards."

We would like to refer the protesting parents to the Supreme Court obscenity decision of June 21, 1973, which established that only if a work as a whole lacked "serious literary, artistic, political, or scientific value" could it be labeled pornographic or obscene by the courts. The Justices also stated that "local standards" could be used to determine the presence or absence of such value. Since we, as longtime members of this community, firmly believe that the book has considerable literary and artistic merit--and since those who favor censorship have never outlined the "standards" that Catch-22 fails to meet--we feel that the burden of proof is on them. In any case, it seems to us that, given the wide critical and popular acceptance accorded Heller's

Figure 13.   Opinion Paper (*cont.*)

novel, it is most unlikely that any court would uphold their position.

Finally, we should like to point out that, like most attempts at censorship, this one has back-fired. Human nature dictates that anything stamped "forbidden fruit" immediately becomes irresistible. We cite the case of the attempt by Jacqueline Kennedy Onassis to suppress certain parts of William Manchester's The Death of the President. The result was a mad rush to buy the magazine version of the book, and when the book itself came out it was an overnight best-seller. And efforts to prevent the sale of critically acclaimed novels with a heavy emphasis on sex, such as Lady Chatterley's Lover by D. H. Lawrence and Tropic of Cancer by Henry Miller, merely guarantee an overwhelming demand for these books. In Langston, the attacks on Catch-22 have produced hundreds of requests for the book at the town library and local bookstores.

In sum, the protestors' actions effectively work against their own cause. More important, their cause has little merit in the first place; and their claim to speak for the community is invalid. The South Langston Citizens Group supports the school board in its decision to retain Catch-22 in its twelfth-grade curriculum.

> South Langston Citizens Group
> Barbara Smith, Chairman

Figure 13. Opinion Paper (*cont.*)

censorship backfiring is off the mark, since it deals with the effects of censorship in general, not the book that is being attacked. Furthermore, from the emotional standpoint mentioning the Manchester case is risky, because many readers might identify with Mrs. Onassis rather than Mr. Manchester.

What makes this opinion paper effective, primarily, are the facts Mrs. Smith brings out and the consistency of her tone. To the two groups of uncommitted readers, and probably to some members of the third group as well, Mrs. Smith sounds like an informed citizen, someone who can relate her feelings to those of others by means of evidence and examples.

Features

The writer preparing a feature for a club or social group newsletter need not place a premium on evidence and examples, but he does have to relate well to people. He acts as both reporter and commentator, describing the group's activities but also trying to stimulate increased interest among members. He is thus informant and persuader to his readers, as well as friend and associate.

In many ways, the feature is very different from other persuasive messages. Whereas the writer of business letters, letters to the editor, and opinion papers is brisk and to the point, the feature writer is casual. His mood is chatty and very friendly. The organization is loosely structured. Club members are frequently mentioned by name.

But the feature writer cannot ignore organization entirely. Nor can he sound too breezy, or he'll end up calling readers' attention to himself rather than to his subject, as in this example:

> Zap! Here's the superwriter with some more info on what's happening around town for all you camera fanatics. Follow me, folks, and learn all about where the action is—photographywise! Hey, and somebody bring the film, please, cuz I forgot it last time and shutter (!) to think about doing that again.

Contrast this bit of prose, more irritating than enjoyable to the reader, with the feature that follows. The latter has a conversational style that captures just the right mood, and the writer has balanced information and commentary. It's colorful, yet restrained.

Roving About

by Jerry Thompson

Someone in my office said it last week: "Hey, it's Spring!"

Evidently photographers don't have to be reminded of that. Shutters have been clicking all over town in the last few days, and lots of photographic activity will inject you with a fresh outlook in the next few weeks. I'll let you click away on your own, but I'd like to tell you about some of the activities.

By all means our own meeting on the 21st gets top priority. Bill Nafsinger will lead off with a discussion of lenses, and Tom Sweeten will wrap up with a presentation on posing. Bill just acquired something with the label TELEPHOTO and undoubtedly will have some interesting comments about that. Tom will project some slides that illustrate what he calls "the over-the-shoulder look." I frankly don't know what that means, but I'm looking forward to seeing his work. He's been developing it, he says, over the last three months.

Been down to the Civic Center this last week? There's an exhibition by Richard Dow there until the 18th. Yes, it's worth seeing! Dow is a texture specialist—very few scenes, lots of closeups with excellent detail. Ever try shooting an old boot? How about a wad of gum? And lucky Dow! Somewhere he found a polystyrene "Mrs. Suburb" doll that comes across terrifically in *low-grain* paper. Go see the prints of it if nothing else.

On your way back from the Center you might stop by the Card and Camera on Main St. Ed Ashcroft, the owner, is having a special this week and next on developing supplies. I ran into Nancy McCarthy there last Thursday, and we both weaved out of the place loaded with boxes. Nancy asked a good question: "Is any of this stuff tax deductible?" Sorry, Nan, I checked later. But enjoy it anyway.

Those of you who are interested in cinema will certainly enjoy seeing *Medium Cool* again. It's the film about the 1968 Democratic convention in Chicago—remember? It's a real lesson in cutting. Some of it is a little jarring, maybe too much so, but on the whole this is the work of a real pro, Haskell Wexler. The film is being shown at the Majestic this week only.

All this activity should keep you busy during the next few weeks. Don't forget to leave yourself some time for shooting though. To revamp an old saying, "In Spring a young man's fancy lightly turns to thoughts of his Yashica Electro 35."

Format, Appearance, Style

Thus far, we have discussed parallels between written and spoken persuasive messages. We turn now to those aspects of the written persuasive message that distinguish it from spoken communications: format, appearance, and stylistic details.

Sometimes people forget that with a written message the format itself (the arrangement of typed material on the page) can help achieve the persuasive goal. Each of the letter formats that follows (Figures 14–17) suits a different persuasive purpose; you should always consider the specific purpose of your letter before deciding which format to use.

Each of these forms will influence a reader differently. The full-blocked letter looks more businesslike and efficient than the other forms (and it certainly is more efficient in terms of reduced typing time). The indented format looks more personable because it is the closest to a personal letter. The varying degrees of informality in between are suggested by the modified block and semiblock. Generally, the full-blocked format makes a complaint letter or letter to the editor more formidable, while the indented works best in a situation where the sender and receiver are good friends.

With messages that are not essentially letters, alternative formats are available. The writer of an opinion paper can arrange the writing on the page to look like a term paper—title centered and so forth—and thus create a scholarly impression. Or he can use the letter format to create a more personal impression. The feature writer generally has the option of a newspaper article format or the letter format. With the former he creates more of an informative impression. With the latter he is more personable. In all of these cases the principle of the format as persuasion applies.

Figure 14.　Full-blocked

　THE PERSUASIVE MESSAGE IN WRITTEN COMMUNICATION

Figure 15.   Modified Block

Figure 16. Semiblocked

Figure 17.   Indented

The second principle that divides the written persuasive message from the spoken one concerns the importance of overall appearance. The sender has to consider such matters as clean typing, stationery, even margins, and so forth. Some good rules:

Use good quality paper.

Use printed stationery whenever you can.

Do not make more than two erasures per page and make sure the erasure is clean.

Have a style manual on your desk to check proper placement of items in various formats.

Keep the right margin as even as possible.

These rules apply as much to off-the-job persuasive messages as to occupational ones. A smudgy letter is as likely to be discarded by your congressman as by a business client.

The third general point about the written persuasive message is that seemingly trivial stylistic details can be significant. Spelling errors, especially, are likely to distract the reader from the point you are trying to make. Minor and major grammatical errors may have the same effect, though most readers have become flexible in recent years. When used with restraint, certain punctuation marks, particularly the exclamation point and the dash, may be of great value; but the sender needs to be cautioned (!) against becoming—an exclaimer—!!!—or dashomaniac!!

Finally, to repeat a point made earlier in the chapter, the persuasive written message can rely heavily on information in order to effect a significant change in the reader's views or promote a specific action. Facts, statistics, and data, in the long run, probably carry as much weight in the average mind as the emotional appeal. And this may be slightly more true of the written message than of the spoken one, because the receiver has a permanent copy of the message to refer back to.

Nevertheless, as we stressed at the beginning of chapter 8, persuasion will not be successful unless the sender has a good insight into the human personality and the way it operates. We'll end this chapter by presenting a sales letter by a man who has obviously learned something about that personality (Figure 18).

Saturday Review

380 Madison Avenue, New York, N. Y. 10017

Dear Subscriber:

(Text omitted at the suggestion of the
Society for the Suppression of
Cheery Renewal Letters.)

Sincerely yours,

George Emerson

George Emerson
For Saturday Review

GE:RBN

P.S. We left out the usual letter, which most people
don't read anyway. Chances are, you don't need to be
reminded that your Saturday Review subscription is up for
renewal. And surely, you don't need to be reminded how
important SR is to your enjoyment of the world of books,
ideas, entertainment and the arts. So make sure your
copies continue without interruption each week -- fill
out and return the enclosed renewal form today.

Figure 18.   Successful Sales Letter

Summary

The persuasive message can be applied to a variety of on-the-job and off-the-job situations. In these situations, the motivational sequence is a valuable aid toward persuading the receiver. For the writer, format and appearance are persuasive and so are minor stylistic details that are easy to overlook. For the writer, as for the speaker, information itself can be a powerful persuasive tool.

Assignments

1. You are driving on a superhighway far from home. You stop for gas and oil, and charge the purchase with your gas credit card. A day later you stop to get gas again and find that the attendant at the service station on the superhighway left the oil cap off the crankcase. As a result oil is splattered all over the engine and the generator is all but burnt out. You have the car fixed, and the total of the bill for cleaning the engine and replacing the generator is $80.

You then write the Director of Highways, asking for the address of the oil company that has the service-station franchise for the superhighway you traveled. He gives you the address and you write the company, directing your letter to the Customer Service Department and enclosing xerox copies of your credit card receipt and the repair bill.

A month goes by with no reply to your letter. Write a second letter to the company that will elicit not only a reply but also a satisfactory settlement of the action. Remember that you want them to know you are dissatisfied with their failure to respond, but that if you sound off at them you may end up with nothing.

2. You are the principal of a high school. You receive a letter of complaint from the father of a member of the football team. He complains that his son is not playing enough. You check

with the football coach, Mr. Diehl, who explains that Mr. Mortenson's son, Bruce, is a good football player, but he has a habit of missing a practice every other week or so. Furthermore Bruce *is* a senior, as Mr. Mortenson has pointed out, but this doesn't guarantee him more playing time than he had as a junior. In fact, the theory is that *juniors* should play more because they need the experience.

Write a letter to Mr. Mortenson explaining what Mr. Diehl told you. Follow the general rules given in this chapter for answering letters of complaint.

3. Clip an ad for a job in your field from a newspaper. Write a letter applying for the position to accompany your data sheet. (Save this letter to use as a model when you actually go job-hunting.)

4. Write an effective sales letter advertising a product or services.

5. Write either a letter to the editor or an opinion paper. Demonstrate that you can do two things: build an effective argument and relate to an audience on its own terms.

6. Write a review of activities in a club you belong to. Make sure you get the right mood.

10
Code

HAVING APPLIED SOME of the basic principles of communication to everyday situations, we return now to the source and significance of those principles, mentioned briefly in chapter 1. Specifically, we deal in this chapter with the crucial factor of *code*.

Code! Remember that in our discussion of the communication process we said that code meant *language*: a system of spoken or written symbols called words. These in turn were arranged in patterns called sentences, patterns that enable people to communicate.

Words: Language as Symbol

Every day we communicate by using thousands and thousands of words, without consciously thinking of them as *symbols* of the things they describe. This is because we have used these words over and over so many times that our minds make the connections automatically, in writing and in speaking.

To understand the significance of words as symbols, imagine yourself suddenly lifted from your everyday sphere of activity into a foreign country. When you try to communicate with someone there, you suddenly find that the words you used for communication in your own country no longer mean anything. You point to a rectangular leather container with a handle, say the word for it—suitcase—and ask that it be taken to your hotel room. You are amazed when the person you are addressing comprehends neither the word nor the sentence pattern into which you have fit it. All along you were assuming that the sound sōot-kās and its corresponding combination of letters, s-u-i-t-c-a-s-e, would be immediately understood. But now you are confronted with the fact that neither the sound nor appearance of the word—assuming you might write it down for your listener—works. What do you do in this case? Probably you point again to the object, repeat your word symbol or show him your written symbol again, and gesture toward the upper floors of the hotel. Repeating this enough times will probably produce the desired result, but it will be a terribly frustrating and exhausting experience.

This kind of situation very quickly suggests the miraculous quality of language. Groups of people, you discover, have been able to agree about the meaning of symbols for various objects, actions, and ideas. They use these symbolic designations to short-cut the kind of effort you just went through. Instead of making elaborate hand gestures and repeating various sounds, instead of drawing diagrams and pictures on paper—they use words!

The Origins of Language

Sitting in your room thinking about this question of code, you may have wondered how the very first word was created—something many people have speculated about. One of the most popular theories holds that speech was derived from involuntary cries expressing emotion—such as a howl when someone burned his hand. Another holds that the first words came about when people imitated the sounds of nature, from animal growls to falling rain.

In any case, the birth of language stimulated the birth of civilization, for it is language that separates man from the animals. Through this system of sound symbols, and later print symbols, man short-cut the actions and gestures by which he had previously communicated. By this system, too, he was able to describe more accurately the variety of feelings and ideas he experienced. Instead of clubbing his mate and dragging her to his cave, he wooed her with a series of sounds—perhaps the first sentence. With the development of language, man became not only more efficient but also more reasonable.

Problems with Meaning

If, however, we jump back to the present, we find that all is not as ideal as, perhaps, it should be. Why? Because these symbols that we have identified as words sometimes cause problems. Some of these symbols have meanings about which we are *not* in agreement. Words to describe objects and simple actions—concrete words—offer little difficulty. If, for example, we disagree about the meaning of *chair, run, TV set,* or *daffodil* we can easily resolve the problem by pointing to the object or demonstrating the action. But other words—abstract ones—offer real problems. How, for instance, can we easily describe such concept words as *liberal, conservative, communism, religion,* and *pleasure?* Practically everyone has a slightly different interpretation of the meaning for each.

There are, then, certain word-symbols about which we are not all agreed. But oddly enough, we sometimes find difficulty in our use of the code arising from word-symbols about which we *are* in agreement. *Pig, honky, nigger, kike,* and *spic* are used by some to mean policeman, Caucasian, Negro, Jew, and Puerto Rican respectively. The simple fact that these sick terms *have* meaning makes them no less distasteful to the people mentioned. They are stigma words, and those referred to inevitably react with hostility toward the person who uses them.

Compounding the issue of meaning is the context in which the word is used: the rest of the words in the sentence, the tone of voice in which it is spoken, the facial expressions or gestures the speaker uses. The sender and receiver may be in agreement about the meaning of a word if the word is isolated. But when it is spoken with a certain inflection, the impact of the statement may be just the reverse of what the words themselves seem to indicate. "You're a *great* conversationalist," you can say to someone, "you're *superb* when you talk." And you may be anything but complimentary.

These problems involving meaning, however, are only a part of the difficulties that surround language. We know, for example, that when we use certain patterns of words in certain places they don't seem to fit. They might have worked in other circumstances, but on these occasions they seem very out of place. All that loosely grammatical talk seemed so appropriate at the student hangout, but in the presence of lawyers and doctors it brings incredulous stares. So you change the code for professional people only to find yourself out of place the next time you have coffee with your close friends.

Another problem occurs when we find ourselves in different regions of a country that uses one language, or in another country that supposedly uses the same language we do. There are places in the United States, according to linguist H. L. Mencken, where it is proper for a mother to "snot that young un" instead of blow his nose.[1] Ironically, it would be extremely bad taste for that same mother to say aloud any word like *ram* or *buck* that refers to the male animal species. Similar language usages and taboos are often the source of amusement—and embarrassment—to travelers in England. There the hood of the car is called a *bonnet*, and a napkin can mean the same thing as a diaper.

A similar problem arises when we start investigating special fields. *Depot* and *magazine* mean something vastly different in the armed services than they do in everyday life. *Fade* and *zoom* are like new words when used by television technicians. On their return to earth the moon astronauts donned BIGs, biological insulation garments, to avoid contaminating the earth's atmosphere with any alien organisms.

The same confusion exists among various subcultures of our overall culture. High school and college students, for example, have a special vocabulary that usually baffles their parents (think of the slang of the late sixties: *uptight, bummer, bad scene, blow your mind,* and *freaked out*). And many of the recent problems involving minority groups in this country can probably be traced to a similar communications gap involving code. Here is an approximate recording by the late Black Muslim leader Malcolm X of a Harlem hustler's dialect:

> Hey, baby! I dig you holding this all-originals scene at the track . . . I'm going to lay a vine under the [three] balls for a dime—got to give you a play . . . Got the shorts out here trying to scuffle up on some bread . . . Well, my man, I'll get on, got to go peck a little, and cop me some z's—

and here is the translation by Malcolm X:

> The hustler had said he was aware that the Muslims were holding an all-black bazaar at Rockland Palace, which is primarily

1. H. L. Mencken, *The American Language* (New York, 1965), pp. 308–09.

a dance hall. The hustler intended to pawn a suit for ten dollars to attend and patronize the bazaar. He had very little money but he was trying hard to make some. He was going to eat, then he would get some sleep.[2]

Obviously, there are several very different "languages" all operating simultaneously in this country (and most others). Not surprisingly, our use of code is a source of many communication problems every day.

Semantics: Understanding Language Difficulty

Just what is one to do when faced with all these problems? A good question. But by no means a hopeless one, because those who make a profession of studying language have come up with some conclusions that suggest ways to improve the situation. These people are called semanticists, and they take a scientific approach to words and their meanings. They are students of psychology and sociology as well as language. They are interested in the words used by advertising personnel as well as the language of a scholar. They study the speech of government officials, laborers —everyone. In the process, they have arrived at some basic conclusions that will enable the average individual to handle code more efficiently.

One of these conclusions you have already encountered: language is nothing more than sound or print symbols. These symbols, semanticists say, are only a means to an end. There is nothing sacred about them in and of themselves. Over the years, the symbols and meanings change as people apply the words in different ways. Sometimes the words seem to gain in value (*nice* once meant "unaware"); at other times the words have declined in prestige (*crafty* once meant only *skilled in handicraft*).[3] Sometimes, as we saw with *depot, magazine, fade, zoom* and *BIGs*, the words are merely extended to fit new developments.

2. Malcolm X, *The Autobiography of Malcolm X* (New York, 1966), p. 310.
3. Simeon Potter, *Our Language* (Baltimore, Md., 1950), p. 113.

Regardless of how the words have changed, in value or form, the concept still applies: language is in a state of minor but constant flux. The writer or speaker, then, should take care to keep up with the changes in his language, and he should try to anticipate difficulties in defining terms. He should also use the most recent edition of the dictionary that is available to him, as a ten-year-old dictionary can sometimes be misleading.

A second conclusion is that, despite the changing nature of language, words in themselves can be identified at a specific time and place in helpful ways. For example, abstract words, such as *liberal, conservative, communism, religion,* and *pleasure,* are all subject to occasional misuse by politicians, who—for the purposes of getting votes—like to reduce such terms to one narrow meaning. Depending on the occasion and the political bias of the user, of course, *liberal* and *conservative* have probably been interchangeably equated with *devil* or *saint.* Such simplistic equations, of course, make no allowance for the degrees of liberalism and conservatism. The definitions vary not only from party to party, but also within the various factions of a party. A person should be wary, then, of people who throw around these abstractions loosely.

Two other terms may also be of help in this matter of identifying specific meanings. These are *denotative language* and *connotative language. Denotative language* refers to the use of neutral words whose meanings derive from dictionary definitions. *Connotative language* refers to emotion-charged words whose meanings have been tinged by the user. As an illustration, here is a newspaper headline in denotative language:

GOVERNOR BROWN ON TRIP TO FLORIDA

And here is the same idea expressed in connotative language:

GOVERNOR BROWN JUNKETS IN SUNNY MIAMI

In the first example the event is reported in a straightforward manner, but in the second the language implies that Brown is spending the taxpayers' money on a pleasure trip.

For further clarification of these terms take a look at these word arrangements:

bigoted, opinionated, biased, committed, concerned
    kissed one another, embraced, flew to each other's arms
went livid, reddened, flushed, blanched
    talented child, prodigy, five-year-old Bernstein, boy genius

The words toward the left and right we might classify as connotative. The ones toward the middle are more neutral and therefore denotative. In the long run, *exactly* which ones are most denotative and connotative will depend upon our judgment of the situation at hand. If you think that a speaker has tried to sway audience feelings with emotional language, then perhaps the adjective you ought to use is *biased*. If *flush* is too mild a term to describe the color of your father's face when he is upset, you could say he *reddened* with anger. If you think that *five-year-old Leonard Bernstein* accurately describes your musical cousin, and that the movie hero and heroine *embraced* rather than *kissed one another*, then you should use those terms. But when you catch yourself consistently using *only* connotative or *only* denotative language, then you should think before you speak: exactly how will my listener interpret the words I use?

What we are saying is that it is difficult to identify *individual words* as being connotative or denotative. But it is possible to look at *combinations* of words and identify them. We are also saying that neither denotative language nor connotative language is, in itself, better than the other. Newspapers, for example, since they are designed to present "just the facts" (except on the editorial page), should make heavy use of denotative language. By the same token, fiction and poetry should rely more heavily on connotative language, since their content is the area of emotions. The important point is that each occasion demands its own proportion of either denotation or connotation. We wouldn't want a daily paper loaded with "charged" words, nor would we want a novel to be neutral in its language to the extent that it was bland. We don't want political speeches to be all flair with no food for thought. Nor would a speaker—political or otherwise—gain many listeners if he offered only substance and no style. A sophisticated approach to language involves the ability to isolate words in their patterns and then judge how they fit the situation.

This brings us to a third conclusion about code, which we have already implied: word meanings are always subject to change according to the context of the situation. How many of us as listeners, for instance, tend to pick up a sentence or two from a person's formal speech and then tear it to shreds, regardless of the rest of the speech that surrounded it? We may be doing the speaker a grave disservice, in order to gratify our own egos. For what we summarize as the speaker's thought may not reflect his opinions at all. In the same way many of us pick out a sentence from a newspaper article and judge the whole story from it. "The paper says there's a recession ahead," we say to one another after reading the morning's *Gazette*, but what the story really said was that one economist predicted a recession. Likewise in our daily activity at work we tend to "pick out" sentences and statements that support our view or make matters more dramatic. "Everson said production's down," one worker will say to another in quoting a supervisor. "Looks like a layoff coming." Actually, Mr. Everson said that a layoff would come only if production dropped 15% below last year's level. He has been quoted out of context.

Perhaps an analogy will help illustrate the importance of context. Everyday we cross intersections with WALK signs. Often we are only halfway across when the DON'T WALK sign flashes on. Needless to say, we ignore the sign and keep on walking; the *context* (our position in the middle of the road) overrides the meaning of the sign. Context should be no less important in determining our reactions to what we hear or read.

Thus far we have considered context mainly from the receiver's viewpoint. The sender, however, must also be conscious of the context of his remarks. He needs to ask himself "Could this statement be misread, misinterpreted?" "What dangers does this statement pose if I do not qualify it extensively?" "Am I going to be misquoted if I say that?" "What tone of voice should I use when I come to this part of my speech?" The burden of responsibility for seeing that the individual pieces of his speech are not at odds with the context as a whole rests with him.

Another conclusion we should remember is that language reflects social levels. In other words, there are words and word patterns that can be classified as educated, standard, and substandard. The three levels are best explained in table form (see Figure 19).

	TYPICAL USERS	GRAMMAR AND SENTENCE STRUCTURE	VOCABULARY
Educated	Lawyers, doctors, educators, executives, high gov't officials	Knowledge of fine points of grammar, varied sentence style	Wide (general as well as specialized), constantly increasing
Standard	White- and blue-collar workers, businessmen, store clerks	Basic knowledge of grammar, occasional slips, functional but regular style	Fairly wide, some knowledge of specialization, increasing but not at educated rate
Substandard	Unskilled workers, illiterates	Regular misuse of grammar with little will to change, very basic sentence structure	Small, very little increase, frequent use of vulgar expressions

Figure 19.   Social Levels of English

In practice, of course, the three basic levels tend to overlap. And while presumably educated speech is most desirable in general, there are times when it might be disadvantageous. For example, if a person uses highly polished language in a home where everyday usage is substandard, then he may have trouble communicating. He should not change his speech pattern to the point of sounding insincere or artificial—a lawyer who tried to use *ain't* and *he don't* would sound absurd—but should simply be somewhat less formal than he normally is. He can afford to loosen up his sentence structure.

By the same token, a person with substandard or low standard usage needs to be very aware of the patterns of standard and educated usage if he intends to move about in places where those are the accepted rule. There his *ain'ts* and *he don'ts* and *can't hardlys* will show. Unlike the heroine of *My Fair Lady*, he may not find his prestige changed dramatically if he changes his speech habits, but over the long period of time, his status will improve.

As is perhaps evident by now, many English texts in the past have been geared to this improvement in personal status by improvement in speech habits. In recent years, however, there has been considerable controversy about the rigidity that characterizes these books. The rules, the critics say, do not necessarily reflect actual speech practices. While we do not intend to get into a full discussion of such matters, it is important to note at least one striking change in thinking: that one accepted standard of usage should not be imposed upon every geographical area and subculture in the country.

What this boils down to is the final conclusion, namely, that there are not only educated, standard, and substandard usages but also an extrastandard usage. In other words, if Southerners speak with a pronounced drawl, if people from Maine say "earl" instead of "oil," if Texans say "thin" instead of "then," these pronunciations *become* the accepted usages in those areas, and are in no way incorrect.

The same reasoning applies to vocabulary as to pronunciation. Student slang, for example, is acceptable in conversation with other students. And the language used by other subcultures, such as minority groups, should not be considered substandard, but rather extrastandard. Clearly, a more accurate graphic illustration of usage levels would include the extrastandard, as in Figure 20.

	TYPICAL USERS	GRAMMAR AND SENTENCE STRUCTURE	VOCABULARY
Educated	Lawyers, doctors, educators, executives, high gov't officials	Knowledge of fine points of grammar, varied sentence style	Wide (general as well as specialized), constantly increasing
Standard (Extrastandard)	White- and blue-collar workers, businessmen, store clerks	Basic knowledge of grammar, occasional slips, functional but regular style	Fairly wide, some knowledge of specialization, increasing but not at educated rate
Substandard	Unskilled workers, illiterates	Regular misuse of grammar with little will to change, very basic sentence structure	Small, very little increase, frequent use of vulgar expressions

Figure 20. Social Levels of English

The Roles of Sender and Receiver in Understanding Language

The foregoing discussion, of course, only scratches the surface of code usage. However, it does help us to answer the two important questions we've been considering all along: What part do the sender and receiver play in the use of language? What are their respective responsibilities?

For the sender the key word is probably caution. Now that he's aware of all the potential difficulties involved with those simple things called words, he needs to ask himself if he has considered each and every one of them with care. Are they too concrete or abstract? What emotional reactions will they produce in the receiver? What level of usage emerges from the total pattern? Is this the right level for the occasion? What will readers or listeners fail to understand because their background is different from his?

The receiver has to think along similar lines. Has he placed the sender's remarks in the context of the speech or written material as a whole? Has he allowed him enough latitude in his use of specialized vocabulary and regional expression? On the other hand, are there general words that might have worked just as well as the special ones? And what about the ideas the speaker or writer has expressed? Is he justified in using that connotative language or is he trying to appeal to your emotions instead of your reason? For the receiver, the key phrase is discriminating flexibility. He needs to know when to be critical.

Both persons should keep in mind that there are millions of words in the English language. It is asking too much for us to be professionals in handling all of them. It is not asking too much for us to be adept with those we commonly use.

Summary

Code means language, and language is a series of symbols by which people communicate. We do not know exactly how the first words and sentences came about, but this process of substituting symbols for actions and responses was partly responsible for the birth of civilization.

We face difficulties with the use of language even today. But many of them can be overcome with the help of semantics, the study of word meanings in relation to language change, context, and social levels of acceptance. The sender and receiver both share certain responsibilities in dealing with code.

Assignments

1. Give a short talk on whether there are too few or too many words in the English language today.

2. Assume you are an advertising writer in a city where the

people have an average education. Write a sales letter to be sent to these people. Then assume you have been transferred by your company to a community where the people are very well educated. Revise the letter so that the language conforms to the accepted level of this new community. Keep the product or services you are selling the same. Change the language.

3. Give a short talk relating your encounters—humorous or otherwise—with regional speech in traveling about the U.S. or elsewhere.

4. Find a paragraph in a newspaper editorial or other piece of writing which is inflammatory because of its connotative language. Revise the paragraph by substituting denotative words and phrases for those that are connotative.

5. Give a short talk on the possibilities of a universal language for the world. What are the chances of English becoming this universal tongue? Support your ideas.

6. If you are in a technical field, write two sets of brief instructions for operating a machine or piece of equipment you might use: a sextant, an oscilloscope, etc. In the first set of instructions, use the specialized vocabulary of your field. In the second set use a more general vocabulary, so that a layman not acquainted with your speciality could understand the instructions.

7. Give a short talk or write a short paper on the value of visual (nonverbal) symbols in one of the following fields: advertising, politics, military life.

8. Go to the library and see what information you can find about the following theories concerning the origin of language: goo-goo, woo-woo, ding-dong, yoo-hee-ho, Tower of Babel, and oral gesture. Explain these theories in an informative talk to the class.

11

The Other Kind of Code

- FACIAL EXPRESSION, BODY MOVEMENTS, TONE OF VOICE

- TIME, SPACE, TOUCH, SMELL, COLOR

- THE OVERSIMPLIFICATION PROBLEM

IN OUR LAST chapter we took up code, which we said meant language. We turn now to a different kind of code, no less significant as a mechanism enabling people to send messages back and forth. This new dimension of communication does not involve a combination of words; rather, it is a kind of "hidden talk" that goes on while people send and receive verbal messages, and even when they are not consciously sending messages at all. By "hidden talk," we mean the language of facial expression, the body movements that accompany speech, and the tone of voice a person uses in talking. In a much broader sense of the term *code,* we refer also to the way time, space, touch, smell, and color speak to us. Roughly half of our communication, some experts estimate, occurs in this nonverbal dimension, the subtle behavior saying as much as our carefully considered words and having just as far-reaching effects.

Facial Expression, Body Movements, Tone of Voice

Let's be more specific, beginning with the three nonverbal factors noted above: facial expression, body movements, and the tone of your voice. Recall the last time a poor salesman tried to sell you a product? His words claimed your attention if you glanced away and just listened to them without watching him, but when you looked him directly in the face, there was no indication that he really believed what he was saying. His eyes lacked sparkle, his jaw verged on a yawn at one point, and his mouth rarely showed enthusiasm. His *face* said: "Well, this product is okay, but I'm not going to go all out for it."

How about body movements? Consider this example. You're sitting in an auditorium, listening to a speech which you are enjoying. You weren't very enthusiastic at first, because the speech is about psychology, which has never been your favorite subject. However, you're finding yourself more and more involved. For one thing the psychologist has outlined her speech in five parts, and every time she comes to a new part she holds up one, two, three, four, or five fingers to indicate where she is in the talk. In other words, she's easy to follow. Not only that, she has a way of visually reinforcing her points about emotional states. When she came to discussing mental breakdown, for instance, she opened her arms wide in a collapsing semicircle around her body, her arms ending limp at her sides. When she talked about how people withdraw, she wrapped her arms about her, strait-jacket fashion. Sitting there watching the woman, you can't help but be absorbed. She's communicating the nature of various mental states by demonstrating them.

That's only part of the reason for your positive reaction. Another reason you're involved is that the woman uses her tone of voice descriptively too. When she explains paranoia, the un-warranted persecution fears that people sometimes have, she talks into the microphone in a conspiratorial whisper—as a para-noid person, afraid that someone is "watching" him, might do. When she talks about manic-depressive mental patients, who alternate between states of extreme sadness and extreme joy, she alternatively half-giggles and half-groans.

What's happening in these two examples? The salesman and the psychologist are speaking to you as much through their facial expressions, body movements, and tone of voice as they are through their words. They're sending messages that reinforce, neutralize, or—in the case of the salesman—even contradict what they are saying. As a receiver you are monitoring all this behavior, while taking in the sender's words.

Time, Space, Touch, Smell, Color

If you're surprised to learn that you've been doing this monitoring as a receiver, we have another surprise for you: you've prob-ably underestimated exactly how much monitoring you do in these day-by-day situations. As proof of that, consider how you constantly monitor time. U.S. Americans (as opposed to their Latin counterparts) are very time-conscious, compartmentalizing time. They feel the need to use minutes and hours for a beneficial purpose. If the salesman dawdled through his presentation, no matter how favorably you reacted to the product, you might not buy it. All through the presentation you might be telling yourself: "He's wasting my precious minutes." Contrast this with the successful salesman, whose presentation moves right along. No matter how illogical his pitch, you probably caught yourself thinking: "This guy's really efficient. If he's that kind of person, he must have a good product."

While you were considering the factor of time, you were probably also keeping track of how much space there was between you and the other person. Edward Hall, author of *The Hidden Dimension,* has said that all of us stake out territorial zones in our everyday activity, and that depending on the circumstances of the moment, we prefer people to be at certain distances from us. Sometimes we prefer them at the more remote *public distance* (twelve to twenty-five feet or more away from us). At other times we prefer them nearer, keeping *social distance* (seven to twelve feet away). Or perhaps we like them close, in the *personal distance* zone (one and one-half to four feet), or the *intimate distance* zone (almost touching to eighteen inches). In the case of the salesman again, it may be that even though his presentation was effective, you were annoyed because he got too close to you, crossing the line between social and personal distance before you were ready for him to make the move. Or perhaps he kept too far away, so that you felt he was being standoffish.

Another way of looking at space, other than in terms of distance, is in terms of placement—where a person positions himself in relation to others. In an auditorium, for example, the speaker—such as the psychologist discussed above—has little choice other than to be in front of the audience, facing rows of individuals. But if the psychologist were in a smaller room with a smaller group, she would have more options to increase or decrease her communicative effectiveness. She could use the same theater-like arrangement, but that might make the occasion seem more formal than she wished. A better option might be for her to request that the group form two semicircles in front of her. That way she is still the center of attention, and the group feels more like a cohesive unit. Applying these same principles to the salesman, consider a situation where he is selling his product to two people, the president of a company and his vice-president. If the salesman consistently positions himself nearer the vice-president, the company president might feel offended, his authority undermined. If, on the other hand, the salesman reverses the position, the vice-president will feel slighted. So the obvious answer for the salesman is to position himself triangle-fashion, an equal distance from both people, so that he seems to have equal respect for both.

At some time during your interaction with the salesman, you may have been monitoring the factor of touch. Sales personnel frequently begin their presentation by shaking hands with you. In so doing, each salesman indicates what kind of person he is: forceful (firm grip but not clutching), outgoing (handshake feels comfortable to both parties), domineering (the bone-crusher), sensitive (the hand responds to your various pressures), and so on. Thus he reveals his personality before he has even started his pitch.

The salesman also might have indicated something about himself by his cosmetic aroma (if any) and the colors he wore. Perhaps he was heavily doused in aftershave lotion. Depending on whether or not you like such products, your reaction to his sales pitch would have been more or less favorable. The same goes for colors. Was he wearing a shocking pink shirt? If you wear more subdued colors—grays, browns, and blues, for example—you would probably interpret his appearance, and therefore his image, as overly aggressive. Was he dressed in a dun-colored business suit? Then you probably were more willing to accept his message.

As is obvious by now, we monitor a great deal, and to ignore these factors and the hidden talk that accompanies them is to cut off part of the code of everyday communication. You can't be a good receiver if you're "deaf" to body gestures, facial expression, time, space, and so on. However, the receiver is not the only one who can profit from awareness of this kind of code, as we have stressed with regard to other aspects of communication. The sender too can use nonverbal language to his advantage.

If you're a person on your way to a job interview, for instance, you can say something significant about yourself to the interviewer before you even open your mouth. How? By being a few minutes early for your appointment. It tells your interviewer that you're punctual and won't waste company time. You're indicating your awareness of business scheduling. "Trivial," you say? Not when you consider that you might be competing with applicants whose qualifications and credentials are equal to yours. If they show up late, or squeeze time by getting there at the very last minute, you might be chosen instead of them—you've given yourself an important edge by getting there early.

Take another situation, one in which you send a message by the way you occupy space. You're a member of a neighborhood citizens' group protesting a zoning ordinance proposal for your area. If the size of your group is rather small, you might persuade others to think you're larger than you actually are just by the way you seat yourself at the city council hearing on the ordinance. If you get there early enough, you can obtain seats at the front, back, and both sides of the council chambers. Then, as different members of your group rise to comment on the ordinance, you'll seem to occupy a larger portion of the room, and both councilmen and other citizens will view you as an important constituency. Contrast this method with sitting together as a group. That identifies you immediately as a special-interest group. It also allows you to be boxed in by others. And your chances of being called on also decrease, since the chairman of the hearing will undoubtedly want to be fair by calling on people in all parts of the room.

Let's try a situation involving touch. You're not getting along with someone who lives with you? Try laying a hand on the person's shoulder for a brief moment. Or, if your relationship with the person is an intimate one, try laying your hand on his or hers at the appropriate moment, during a lull in the tension. In our society, where physical contact is not encouraged as much as it is in other cultures, touch has an unexpected way of breaking down barriers that words can't penetrate.

The Oversimplification Problem

These examples show how both sender and receiver can use hidden language effectively. They prove again that this kind of code can be an important factor in your daily communication. But in thinking about nonverbal code, you should try to see it in the proper perspective—this area of communication study is far more intricate than our brief survey indicates.

A lot of recent books and magazine articles tend to oversimplify the factors we've described above. They encourage making snap judgments about a person, on the basis of his posture, facial expression, gestures, and so on. They suggest, for example, that a person sitting with his arms folded on his chest is taking that position to tell you that he's not listening to you. They imply that you can be a more effective leader by using three easily memorized hand gestures when speaking. Unfortunately, such distorted views of the potential impact of nonverbal communication factors are not at all uncommon.

We urge you to read popularized discussions of nonverbal code very carefully, because it is a relatively new science, not yet fully explored. Facial expressions, tone of voice, body movements, time, space, touch, smell, and color *do* influence the act of communication. But when sending or receiving a message, you should not permit these factors to override the considerations we have analyzed in previous chapters. Verbal and nonverbal codes complement one another, often in complex ways. When you communicate, open your mind to all the possibilities of meaning, and see to it that words and hidden talk work together.

Summary

Though words may be the most obvious kind of code, nonverbal communication conveys as much meaning as the language we speak or write. A person's facial expression, tone of voice, body movements, use of time, space, touch, smell, and color tell us a great deal. The receiver and sender regularly monitor the complex hidden talk.

Assignments

1. Watch only the video portion of a political speech on TV. Note which gestures the speaker uses most effectively; which least effectively. Write a paragraph discussing your findings.

2. Discreetly listen to two people conversing. Take notes on how the sound of their voices changed the meaning of what they said. In a small group discussion, compare your notes with those of other students in the class.

3. Spend a whole day without your watch and without looking at a clock. Report to your class how your view of daily life changed, if at all.

4. Have dinner with a friend. Deliberately set some object of yours (purse, cigarette lighter, etc.) on his part of the table, moving it more and more into his territory while you pick it up, use it, and put it back. Watch his reactions and record your observations, later, in a paragraph or two.

5. Keep a three-week record of where people sit in your classes. Do they tend to change places? to keep the same seat? For what reasons? Does the seating arrangement make any difference as to who participates most often in class discussions? Is there a correlation between classroom position and classroom leadership? Give a short talk documenting your opinions.

6. The next time you go out with your spouse or a friend of the opposite sex, wear aftershave lotion or perfume. Does your wearing this make any difference in your communication with each other? (Note: If you regularly wear aftershave lotion or perfume, then try this experiment by not wearing any for a change, and note the results.)

7. Study the seven photographs on the following page. Choose the four expressions that you think best suggest these mental states: alertness, determination, arrogance, and aggression. Be prepared to explain why you have matched a particular photograph with a particular description.

Photos courtesy of Brooks Caldwell

12

Interference

WHEN YOU HEAR the word *interference* mentioned in connection with communication, you may think first of those minor annoyances that distract both sender and receiver: a clicking pencil in a classroom, a smudged, unreadable typing blot on a letter, a loud cough in an audience.

We don't want to belittle these external distractions. They do hinder communication, and they are a very real kind of interference. However, this chapter deals with another kind: *internal* interference, the receiver's tendency to distort the sender's message in accordance with his personal view of reality. This interference is no more intentional than the distractions mentioned above, but it is just as likely to result in poor communication.

The reason for this interference is simply that no two persons think alike. A sender may get off on the wrong foot in communicating a message because he can't anticipate something in his receiver's background or experience that will interfere with his communication. A receiver may suddenly "tune out" on a sender without even realizing he is doing it, because he has a closed mind on the issue being discussed. All of us frequently distort messages by filtering out things we find disagreeable, imposing elements we think should be included, and in general changing the shape of the message to fit our mental image of the world.

Three Illustrations

Now let's examine some typical situations involving this kind of interference. The first takes place in a school, probably somewhat like your own.

A teacher, Mrs. Jennings, is sending a note to Tom Simon, who is responsible for duplicating classroom materials for the teachers. Mrs. Jennings is thinking as she writes to Tom that she has to have an article duplicated for her students by the following afternoon. The article is crucial to the lesson, as a final proof of the point she has been emphasizing during the preceding weeks.

She puts that thought on paper:

Tom,
    I've been working on a good government unit, which I'd like

to finish tomorrow. I need the accompanying article as the final clincher for what I've been stressing.

"Does that say enough?" she asks herself. "Well, no," she thinks, "because I haven't said how many copies I want." She adds:

I'll need 60 copies.

Then a final paragraph:

I know you're busy, and I hate to ask, but can I have this on a rush basis?

She sends the note and article to Tom via interdepartmental mail. Tom gets them that afternoon, reads the note, and sends it back with his own short reply jotted on the bottom:

I'll get to it. Don't worry about it.

But when Mrs. Jennings shows up the next afternoon, an hour before her scheduled class, she discovers that the article has not been duplicated. Tom is out and will not be back until much later. Crushed, angry at Tom, she leaves the duplicating center feeling betrayed. "He promised," she tells herself. "He said he'd finish the job in time!"

A sad situation. Mrs. Jennings thought she sent Tom the following message: *I need the article by tomorrow afternoon. Can I have it by then?* Tom thought the message *he* sent to Mrs. Jennings said, "I'd finish the job by the end of the week." Obviously, neither receiver interpreted the sender's message as the sender intended him to. What are some possible sources for this confusion?

The main problem is that neither sender was able to anticipate the kind of interference that would distort the receiver's understanding of his message. One element that might be involved here is the difference in age and experience between Tom and Mrs. Jennings, and their mutual failure to recognize the other's priorities. Tom is in his late forties and has worked in the school duplicating center for fifteen years. He's become an established figure on the staff, and he feels he knows how to run his facility efficiently. Roughly half the work orders he gets every day are marked "RUSH," and he's learned over the years that "rush" can usually be interpreted "sometime this week." Therefore, when he promises someone he'll "get to" a rush job, he means he'll have it ready by Friday. He knew Mrs. Jennings was only a first-year teacher, just out of college, and he saw no reason why her "rush" order should be more important than anyone else's.

In addition, he got her note in midafternoon, when he was swamped with work and tired from a long day. Completing her job by the next day would have meant staying late tonight, and he wanted to get home and relax. So his mind took care of the conflict for him, by blacking out the connection between the government class and the xeroxing job—not hard to do, since the note did not make the connection explicit anyway.

Mrs. Jennings simply was not aware that midafternoon was a bad time to hand Tom a rush job, and that the word "rush" should always be accompanied by a specific day and hour to ensure completion before the end of the week. If she had been around longer, she would have known enough to give Tom the job first thing in the morning, with a note stating "Noon, tomorrow" as the desired time of completion. As it happened, Tom filtered out the entire first paragraph of her message.

In writing her a reply, he made the same kind of error that she had with the original note: he *assumed* that a general comment about his intention to do the job would be enough. What he forgot was that, unlike more experienced faculty members, she had no way of knowing that "I'll get to it" was his way of saying "I'll finish it by Friday."

The setting for our next example is a room in a municipal building. A small group of people are gathered in it, listening to a man named Smith. Mr. Smith is in the process of going over a large map, pointing out various locations on it, as he has been doing for some twenty minutes. "And so," he says to the audience, "tentatively, we on the City Planning Board feel the logical place for the new expressway is here, along Barchester

Avenue. As I've tried to say, that will cost the city the least amount of money and will give us the traffic flow that we've needed so long." He steps away from the map, adding that he will gladly hear any reactions from the citizens who came to hear his presentation.

Immediately a lot of people are on their feet trying to get the floor. The first who succeeds is a man named Barzini. "I'm an Italian-American," he says, "and I just want to say one thing. I think it's awful the way you people have decided to tear up our neighborhood this way. That expressway's going right through the middle of the Italian-American district, and it's going to make a lot of us mad. We've got friends who are going to get moved out, you're going to break up our park on Second Street, and worst of all that little restaurant on Fairchild will have to go. A lot of us have been meeting in that place for twenty years. I just don't know how you could do that to anybody." He sits down, furious.

The second person to speak is a Miss Mitchell, stern-looking, middle-aged. "I wonder if you've given any thought," she says, "to the effect all this new traffic will have on church services in that area you're talking about. I've gone to the Catholic church on Barchester Avenue for as long as I can remember, and the services have always been peaceful. I hate to think what attending Mass would be like with trailer trucks going by just around the corner. Sounds to me as though the city wants all its churches to move out to the suburbs."

As soon as she sits down, a man in his early thirties gets on his feet. "I don't suppose I have to introduce myself," he says. "You people from city hall have seen me often enough. Tonight, though, I want to say that in terms of saving money, this expressway is a travesty. Who's going to pay for it? The blue-collar workers in this city, that's who. As though state and federal taxes don't gouge them enough, you want to raise their city taxes sky-high for something that doesn't even do them any good. Those who will really benefit—the factory owners and store owners downtown—have so many loopholes to crawl through their taxes won't be affected at all. Well, this time you're not going to get away with this. We'll mobilize. We'll fight you all the way on this one!" He sits down angrily, barely able to control his rage.

Two more people get up to speak. One is a businessman. Unlike the previous respondents, he speaks in a friendly tone. "I represent the Downtown Development League," he says, "and I'd like to commend the Planning Board for its foresight. I don't think the expressway will affect taxes significantly. I do think the plan will be an economic boon to the downtown area, and I'd like to commend Mr. Smith for his leadership in that direction."

The last person to speak is a Mrs. Perez, who identifies herself as an art historian. She is a small woman, but her voice is rich and carries well, so that she commands full attention. "I just can't understand," she says, "how you people on the commission can overlook the fact that in putting the expressway there, you'll be tearing up three of the most important architectural landmarks in this city. I'm surprised, frankly, that you could even consider tearing up the Templin Building, the Wright Park monument, and the MacKenzie Arcade. I just can't see how any new expressway is worth the price of that destruction."

We've focused on this situation because it illustrates other aspects of the interference problem. But before we turn to them, notice that Mr. Smith, the sender, is pretty bewildered when everyone has finally had his say. He thought his message was a simple one: the planning commission chose the route for the expressway because the route was the most economical and feasible for speeding up traffic. "Furthermore," he thinks, "the plan is only tentative at this point. I made that clear." Evidently, though, people have chosen to interpret his message in ways he did not at all intend.

The first receiver, Mr. Barzini, has taken the message as an attack on his ethnic background—the city is out to get the Italian-Americans. The second receiver, Miss Mitchell, has put the whole message in the context of her religious practices. To her the city's plan is a threat to her spiritual well-being. The next two receivers, the angry young man and the businessman, have yanked the message into the spotlight of sociology and economics. The young man sees the plan as an attack on the poor, the businessman sees it as a boon to the downtown merchants. As he listened to each respondent, Mr. Smith wondered how on earth they could have drawn such conclusions—he didn't even mention the areas that concern them. As for the art historian's contention, it certainly never dawned on Mr. Smith that the expressway plan might be viewed as a deliberate attempt to destroy major architectural landmarks.

Understandably, Mr. Smith is dismayed. "It's as though all of these individuals were filming in their minds what I was saying," he thinks, "and whenever they chose to, they just inserted some scenes I never intended. That guy Barzini had in his mind some movie about Italian-American families being driven from their homes. Miss Mitchell probably saw me with a brass band playing in front of her church every Sunday. Those next two guys saw me as either an evil slum landlord or a John D. Rockefeller come to save the city. And Mrs. Perez, she probably thinks I'd drive a bulldozer straight into the Washington Monument if I got the chance—wow!"

Mr. Smith, who is new on the Planning Board and has almost no public relations experience, is discovering how easy it is for most people to distort a seemingly simple message. His message, unlike that of Mrs. Jennings, was not filtered out; rather, people imposed their backgrounds onto it. The end result, however, was the same. His information and ideas never came across as he intended. The ethnic, religious, economic, social, and esthetic biases of his receivers interfered to prevent the transmission.

Our third situation takes place in an apartment, on a hot summer evening. A young man, Fred, has invited a young woman, Sarah, over for dinner. It is their first date. Fred noticed Sarah in his accounting class some weeks ago, got interested in her, and overcame his shyness to strike up a conversation. It was a short one, but at the end of it he got her to accept his offer of dinner. Sarah had noticed Fred's interest fairly soon and thought she might be interested in return. When he invited her for the evening, she thought she knew him well enough to accept.

The two people are seated across from each other at the dinner table. They are in the middle of the dessert, and they have been enjoying their new acquaintance. Having finished half a bottle of wine, too, they are more relaxed than they were at the beginning of the meal.

The temperature in the apartment is high—remember it is a warm summer evening—and Sarah says, "Am I ever hot!"

Fred puts the last bit of his piece of pie in his mouth, smiles because it tastes so good, and says, "I can fix that." He gets up, thinking that he will turn on the air conditioner, which is directly behind Sarah.

Before he gets two steps in that direction, however, Sarah is on her feet. "No, you won't!" she suddenly shrieks. "You won't touch me!" She throws her napkin at Fred and dashes out of the apartment, leaving him dumbfounded with his jaw dangling further from the rest of his head than it's ever been before.

Alas, poor Fred. His was a simple message, he thought: *I'll turn up the air conditioner.* But to poor Sarah, who didn't know the air conditioner was behind her, the message was SEDUC-TION! She had heard and read a lot recently about how women were used as sex objects. It was clear to her that men were taking advantage of her sex—all you had to do was look at a few magazine and television ads where the old cheesecake was being used to sell new cars, cigarettes, and even office furniture. Well, she wasn't going to let herself be used! Fred would pay for his arrogance in jumping to conclusions about her word *hot*. She'd never speak to him again!

Unknowingly, of course, Sarah has let her years of exposure to common sexist attitudes interfere with what Fred has tried to say. As a receiver, she has warped the basic shape of his message. Her response to that message has been expressed not only in verbal language, but also in body language, and either way she has indicated her total misinterpretation.

Whether Fred could have grasped the reason for Sarah's words, much less her actions, is a debatable point. But whether he figures out what angered her or not, one thing at least the episode has made clear to him: when people try to communicate, a lot of explosive human chemistry can get in the way, and a message that seems perfectly plain to one person can be loaded with dynamite for another.

Overcoming Interference

All of these examples focus on a central theme: the fact that interference, though it may take several different forms, is likely to complicate any communication situation. But the problem is not usually as disastrous as it was in the case of Fred and Sarah; most people manage somehow to send and receive messages well enough to relate to a wide variety of situations and individuals every day.

How they do that is not an easy question to answer, but we can offer some reasonable explanations, we think. For one thing, when these people are in the role of senders they follow closely a rule discussed in chapter 2: *Learn to anticipate difficulty*. They know that any two people trying to communicate with each other are taking off from different starting lines. They remind themselves frequently that the outcome of a communication situation is never entirely predictable. For this reason the messages they send are as complete and precisely worded as possible.

As we noted in our first example, both Mrs. Jennings and Tom would have done well to keep this rule in mind. Similarly, Mr. Smith failed to anticipate the various concerns that would affect the reactions of his audience. His message emphasized the city budget and the traffic flow, and he failed to stress the tentative nature of the plan. A better approach would have concluded with the following statement, or something like it: "And so at this point the Planning Board feels that the logical place for the new expressway is here, along Barchester Avenue. However, I'd like to point out that this is only a tentative conclusion. And it's a conclusion based only on economic considerations— the least expensive way to speed up traffic in this area. We haven't considered other factors yet; how the plan would affect surrounding neighborhoods, for instance, or stores and factories downtown. We're here to get your thinking on those points too."

As we've already noted, however, the receiver's role in eliminating interference is no less crucial than the sender's. First of all, the receiver should hold back on his conclusions until he has heard or read the whole message. And he should try not to make "flash judgments" on the motives behind a certain message. With no evidence aside from the message itself, as our examples have indicated, it's often hard to tell exactly what's inside someone else's mind. Before deciding *why* someone is making a particular remark, it's a good idea to question him until we have the full story. In other words, the skilled receiver knows he cannot fully understand a message without also becoming a sender—asking questions or writing inquiries until the issue is entirely clear to him. By forcing the original sender to restate the message in more carefully worded language and in a variety of ways, the receiver increases the chances of the message getting through as the sender intended, and ensures a real exchange of information or views.

Applying this discussion to our examples, we can see how the communicators might have done a better job. Tom could have called Mrs. Jennings to clarify her message and explain his own position: "Look, practically everybody who comes in here for duplicating service wants it done on a rush basis, so it's pretty hard for me to finish a big job like yours in one day. But tell me exactly when you need the copies, and I'll see what I can do." In this way their misunderstanding might never have occurred.

The meeting about the new expressway is a better illustration of the problems posed by "flash judgment" interference. If the receivers in this case had listened with open minds, they would not have missed the point about the expressway plan being tentative; and they would have asked just how tentative a plan it was. After hearing Mr. Smith's answer, they would not have envisioned the plan as an attack on their particular area of interest (or, in the businessman's case, as a move in his favor). They might have presented their views to Mr. Smith as follows:

MR. BARZINI: Are you aware of how closely knit our Italian-American community is along your expressway route? Do you realize how upset people might feel about this plan?

MISS MITCHELL: I don't want to jump to conclusions, so I'll ask you how this plan will affect noise in that area. Am I going to be able to hear the priest during Mass on Sunday morning? The expressway will be just around the corner, and that will mean a lot of traffic, which creates a lot of noise . . .

THE YOUNG MAN: Look, can I assume you've made some study of the consequences of the plan for city taxes? Can you tell me what kind of burden the expressway will place on the lower-middle-class residents? Will most of the cost be borne by downtown businesses?

THE BUSINESSMAN: I don't know whether this was your intention, but the plan looks to me like an economic boon for the downtown merchants I represent. If they had to absorb the cost of the expressway, however, it might be a different story.

MRS. PEREZ: I'd like to know what provisions you've made for preserving three significant architectural landmarks in the area you've outlined. Are you going to move the Wright Park monument and the MacKenzie Arcade? What about the Templin Building? I think all of those things are worth preserving, and I wonder what the Board's opinion is.

With these reactions from his audience, Mr. Smith might not have felt so personally attacked. As a result he would have been better able to answer questions and offer additional information. And his receivers would have been able to understand the message as he intended them to.

We've presented possible solutions to the interference problems encountered by Mr. Smith and Mrs. Jennings. Sarah and Fred—well, that's another case. But all three examples illustrate one basic source of interference: a failure to *think* about a message before deciding what it means.

Summary

Interference, the unintentional distortion of a message, results from hidden factors in any communication situation. The message may be distorted because the receiver filters something out of it, imposes something upon it, or changes its basic shape. The reasons for interference are as complex as the differences between two people—their social, economic, psychological, esthetic, and religious attitudes, among many others. Senders can overcome interference by anticipating what the receiver may not understand. Receivers can overcome it by avoiding flash judgments on the message, and by asking questions that clarify the sender's meaning.

Assignments

1. Give a two-minute talk describing a situation in which two people you know successfully overcame interference between them.

2. Clip a cartoon from your newspaper. Explain in a written paragraph to your instructor how two characters in the cartoon are taking off from very different starting points in their attempt to communicate.

3. Give a short talk on some aspect(s) of interference that this chapter does not deal with.

4. The emphasis of this chapter has been on how the differences between people affect their ability to communicate. Write one or two paragraphs explaining how similarities between people influence their communications.

5. In a five-to-seven-minute talk explain some of your experiences traveling in a different part of the U.S. or in a foreign country. Focus on the cultural differences that affected your ability to communicate.

6. Following these assignments is a photograph (see page 210). On a sheet of paper list all the valid assumptions you can make about the scene in it.

7. Give a short talk about some new interest you have taken up in recent months. Explain how that interest has generated other experiences for you.

8. We did not explain how Fred and Sarah might have overcome their interference problem. Do you think the bad ending of the episode could have been avoided? Write a paragraph explaining how.

Index*

*Page numbers in italics refer to sample or illustrative material.

Research report (*continued*)
96; quotations in, 101; sample,
105–17; topical outline for, 98
Résumé. *See* Personal data sheet

S

Sales letters. *See* Business letters
Semantics, 179. *See also* Language,
Meaning
Sender, 12–20
Slang, 184
Speech: audience analysis, 62–63;
conclusion of, 78–79; determining
specific purpose of, 61–67; informative, 60–80; introduction
of, 69–76; persuasive, 119–40;
transitions in, 76–78

T

Tact, and good communication, 11

U

Usage, levels of, 183–85

W

Words, and meaning, 176. *See also*
Code, Communication, Language